MY HIT PARADE

...and a Few Misses

by
Russell
Arms

MY HIT PARADE
...and a Few Misses

by
Russell
Arms

BearManor Media
2005

My Hit Parade...and a Few Misses

For information, address:

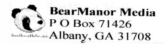

BearManor Media
P O Box 71426
Albany, GA 31708

bearmanormedia.com

Cover design by John Teehan

Typesetting and layout by John Teehan

Published in the USA by BearManor Media

ISBN—1-59393-024-0

Table of Contents

Chapter 1

In the Beginning

I was born in a big house on Russell Street in Berkeley, California on February 3, 1920; family legend says that was how I got my name. They were having a hard time deciding what I should be called when someone glanced out the window and saw the street sign. I instantly became Russell! Not that I remember any of it, but Mom told me later that I was born just after midnight, and so came out an Aquarian. Maybe I'm chauvinistic, but I've always thought that is the best sign.

I have a number of yellowing snapshots showing a solemn-faced little kid playing with a hose on the front lawn or riding a hobbyhorse on that same lawn or just sitting on a cement block with a number of ladies in their old-fashioned dresses hovering about me—Mom, of course, along with my Aunt Betty and my Grandma Emmy. Also present were my Uncle Cortland, and my slightly older brother, Walter. Unfortunately, I never really got to know Walter as we never lived together for any length of time. That's about all I remember about Berkeley.

My dad worked for Crown Zellerbach Paper Co. and was transferred about that time to South Pasadena where we lived for two years. I have further family pictures showing us at the beach with me in a rental bathing suit and Dad sitting in the sand with a high-collar shirt, suit and tie, and topped by a straw hat, looking ludicrous indeed, at least by today's standards. There are also studio-type pictures of me and brother Walter, Mom (looking very stressed), and Dad looking very stern and serious, all making up a very unhappy-looking family.

It must have been true, because it wasn't too long before there was a divorce and that, in those days, was a most serious matter. People just

1

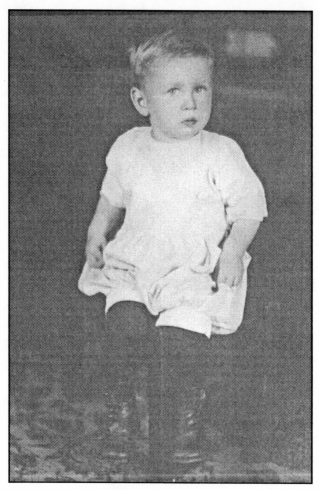

Russie Baby at 3 years.

didn't get divorces at that time. But I'm glad they did because if there ever were two people entirely unsuited for each other it was my mom and dad. I loved them both dearly, but they just should not have been together. She was sweet and fun-loving but entirely smothered by a Victorian-age gentleman who, though he loved her, didn't have the slightest idea of how to show that love in a "proper" manner. But, what am I saying! If they hadn't gotten together, I wouldn't have been here to write this. Ha, maybe that would have been all right, too!

I'll get on with the results of the divorce, but I must relate one story about me in those days. I don't actually remember this, but Mom swore it was true, so guess it is. It seems that if I were scolded sharply or otherwise chastised, I would retire to the next room, go behind the door and PEE! Guess I showed them! She never told me what punishment I got for that, but it couldn't have been too bad as I apparently continued to do it! (I don't do it now, though!)

Anyway, when the divorce happened, Walter and I went with Dad who had been transferred back to San Francisco. He rented a small house in San Mateo, one of the "bedroom" communities adjacent to the city, hired a housekeeper for us, a gal named Louise, and we quickly became a small family. The thing I most remember about Louise is a prayer she taught me. After I said the Lord's Prayer, I would then go on to say: "Angels are God's thoughts passing to man . . . Man is not sick because Mind is never sick, so man cannot be. Thou shalt have no other gods before me. Truth is spiritual, God is Love." I have said that my whole life—kind of a mantra or something, I guess.

I have to interject right here that Mom was devastated by having to "give up" her sons, but in those days it was extremely difficult for a woman alone to make her way, and she was afraid that she wouldn't be able to care for us properly, so thought that leaving that up to Dad was the best way. The decision was to haunt her for the rest of her life, but I didn't particularly notice the difference at that time because I was one of those cute little boys everyone loved!

Family portrait - Russ, Dad, Mom, Brother Walt.

We lived in that house for a couple of years when Dad decided to put Walter in a military school. Of course, I wanted to go along with my brother but I was only four and it took some heavy negotiations with the commandant of the school before he agreed to accept me as a "special" student. Further snapshots show four-year-old-me in a soldier suit looking like a toy soldier next to the rest of the student corps. But it was all fun and games to me, and I was allowed to roam around the school grounds and go into classrooms as I wished. Finally, however, they decided that if I were going to be in a class I might as well take the schooling, so I actually started my education at four years of age.

I don't really remember too much about Palo Alto Military Academy other than shinnying up ropes in Phys. Ed class and being terrified one night when a big thunderstorm hit and I jumped out of bed and ran down a long, dark hallway to the commandant's room where his wife was sitting in a big chair in a pool of light. I took one mighty leap from the doorway and landed in her lap where she comforted me until I stopped shaking and then sent me back to bed. Funny the things that stick in your mind!

We transferred to Menlo Park Military Academy after a couple of years when Major Park and wife moved there. I do remember more about the school because I was a bit older. I got promoted to corporal and then sergeant, and, at age nine, had my "own" squad to command. Pretty snazzy, huh? We drilled with wooden rifles and I do remember a scary incident with those rifles. Major Park had a son about my age with whom I roomed. One day, as we were marching on parade, his boy was out of step or something minor when all of a sudden, the major leaped into the ranks, grabbed the boy, and proceeded to whale the tar out of him with his wooden rifle! Then we continued to march as though nothing had happened. Of course the whole company was "shook!"

I remember another time when I was the victim. I was turned over my bed and beat with a ping pong paddle for telling a fib about something. It hurt but was a lesson well-learned! We also had to sit at attention at mealtime until commanded to eat, and then had to eat every single thing on the plate or the whole company sat there until you did. Actually, it sounds a whole lot worse than it really was. Our major wasn't a tyrant, but he did insist on discipline and saw to it that orders were carried out. Maybe a bit of that might be good in today's society.

Incidentally, in spite of the fact that I had wound up in a military school because I wanted to be with my brother, I saw very little of him

Russ (4 years) and Walt at Palo Alto Military Academy.

because of the four-year difference in our ages. So I guess we started drifting apart about here. We never did become close in our entire lives—just a kind of feeling that we were brothers but it wasn't very important. I really am sorry that happened and wish it could have been different.

On month-ends we were allowed to see our folks. Dad used to come down, and almost every time we did the same thing: took a ride through the Stanford University campus and then went to what was then called a "creamery" where we would have a milk shake (but without the syrup, please!). I grew to look with dread on those little outings, maybe because of the routine. Dad did his best but his sense of discipline made it difficult for him to relax with his kids, resulting in us not having any fun. I think I may have inherited some of that feeling and perhaps that was part of the cause of my divorce from my second wife, Barb, and her two kids. That Victorian sense of discipline!

Mom was different. She missed us a lot but couldn't come down to see us, as she had no car, so we'd take the train into San Francisco, take a trolley to the Ferry Building, and she'd meet us there. She always had a big sack of old bread with her, and we had a great time on the ferry feeding that bread to the sea gulls...a big treat! We went over to Berkeley where she lived in an apartment while working as a dental assistant, and we'd stay overnight only to reverse our trip back to Menlo Park, again carrying a big sack of old bread!

By the time I was ten, Dad had met a new lady, Edith, and was getting very serious about her. She was somewhat younger than he, was an accomplished pianist and had a vibrant personality, also a daughter named Georgene. In due time they were married and he built her a new house in Burlingame, another of the "bedroom" towns for San Francisco. Now, Walter didn't care for Edith, or her daughter, and that made it a bit difficult to decide on family living arrangements. (Me, I got along with everybody.) So, it was decided that Walter would live with Mom who now lived in a rented house in Marin County, which he did.

Our little family in Burlingame was doing fine, as long as the ground rules were followed. Edith used to love to take the train to meet Dad in the city for a night on the town and so I, now the oldest as Walter had chosen not to live with the family, would be in charge of getting dinner for Gege and myself. That was fine until Edith delivered my half-brother, John, which called for a live-in housekeeper, Julie, who added to our growing family. That eased my housekeeping duties a lot when Edith was gone as Julie did the cooking. However, I was happy I did learn to cook 'cause in later years it would come in very handy, as I did a lot of it.

But there was one wonderful treat that I was quick to take advantage of. I mentioned that Edith was an accomplished pianist and she used to practice literally for hours on end. That's a whole other story—remember my father was a Victorian gentleman!—as she was taking out her emotional frustrations on the piano. So, as she played her heart out, I lay on the floor directly under the parlor Steinway and absorbed all of the wonderful, exciting classical music she was pounding out. What an education, what a thrill!

So, life was fine for me. I was in grammar school and active in the Boy Scouts and found a group of fellas to pal around with, and that's the way things went until I graduated and entered high school...at 12 years of age!

I had no trouble with my classes, but when I tried to get into the athletic program, that was a different story. I had the ability to be on the track team, and even on the football team in spring practice, but my body just wasn't developed enough to compete with guys who were at least two years older, and bigger than I. It was frustrating but, even so, I did all right in track and won many events in competition with our local schools. I specialized in the high jump, the pole vault, and ran the 100-yard dash. I also filled in with the broad jump and the low hurdles, when needed, but I couldn't make it in distance events.

As part of the training regime we had to run mile laps, at the end of which, I would inevitably fall on my face in the infield of the track and THROW UP...big time! So I knew that distance races and football were not for me! However, I was rescued by my discovery of THE THEATRE! My accidental discovery of what proved to be my life's work.

Chapter 2
School Days

I never should have been in "show business" in the first place, but, apparently, Someone had other ideas for me. In high school we were told one day that we must take one more course in order to have enough credits to graduate, and they provided us with a short list of courses from which we might choose. I had no idea which to choose until my best friend came along and suggested we might both enroll in Drama One. Little did I know how that lightly-taken decision would change my life!

The first day I walked into class I had a strange feeling that I had come "home." That may sound melodramatic, but it's the truth. Mrs. Janice Robison, our teacher, probably had a lot to do with that. From the first day, she made the class something special and it only got better as the year went on.

I discovered feelings in myself that I didn't know were there, as I was actually very shy. But I found that I wanted to take part in everything that went on and to be a part of all the class activities even though that meant getting up in front of the class and reciting or offering an opinion or whatever. It wasn't easy but I made myself do it and found that people really listened and, best of all, I actually enjoyed doing it!

Burlingame High School was (and still is) a wonderful school. For their time (this was 1932 to 1936), they were very progressive in their thinking and very helpful to the students. The drama department produced two shows annually, a play and a vaudeville show. My first appearance on a stage was in the vaudeville show of 1935. My friend, Dick, and I were to sing "Ragtime Cowboy Joe" while leaning against a fake rail fence and dressed in cowboy garb. Somehow, we managed to get through it, just before I rushed offstage to throw up! So I didn't know if we were a hit or not, but I couldn't have care less because I had just made a real appearance on a real stage! Even through all my retching I had a feeling of triumph and knew I had stumbled into something that I loved!

Things got a little better from then on. That year they were to do the Maxwell Anderson costume drama, *Elizabeth and Essex*, and I, of course, desperately wanted to play the lead part of Essex. Seeing that I was only 14 and the leading lady was 16, it was a bit difficult to convince Mrs. Robison that I should get the part, and I didn't. However, "Robby" did cast me...as The Fool! Maybe that was a portent of things to come! She did tell me that my reading for Essex had been excellent but that I was just too young for the role. Cold comfort for a dedicated young actor, but, what the hey, I did have a part, and the fun of being in a real play made up for everything else. And, this time, I didn't even throw up!

In the meantime, I studied and read and worked hard at everything we did in class and tried to grow up very fast. I must have succeeded because the next year I got to play the part of Death in the play *Death Takes a Holiday*. Now *that* was a part to savor! I still love the play to this day and would quote some very favorable reviews here if only I could remember them. Honest, they were wonderful and, anyway, modesty forbids!

We had a great group of actors in that show, all personal friends, and, best of all, we were all going on to junior college in San Mateo (now College of San Mateo) so we could continue our acting careers together. This we did in such shows as *Stage Door*, *And So to Bed* (about Samuel Pepys in early London), *The Dover Road*, and, best of all, *Craig's Wife*, a heavy drama about a domineering wife, and I got to play the husband— all pretty heady stuff for a young man who had now decided that he would become a famous Broadway actor!

In 1937 (I was 17), I did get some real work in "show business." I had gone up to radio station KFRC in San Francisco to audition as an actor, as the station produced several live radio dramas each weekend. However, remember this was before there were any unions in radio. I did get hired and actually did a number of parts, maybe three or four roles over a Saturday and Sunday, and I would be paid—whatever they had left over that week! So, I was always surprised the next week when I went into collect my check. One week it might be $9.25 and the following week it could be $14.62. I didn't care because I was actually working as an actor. And being *paid*?!

Russ in *Death Takes a Holiday* at Burlingame HS, 1935.

Later on, I remember KFRC did a show called *The Phantom Pilot*, and I was assigned to play the pilot. All well and good—except that after only about four weeks (for which I got $25 per show), they moved the show down to Los Angeles! Oh well, I had my moment of glory. I did this for two years in junior college and really enjoyed it, as it made me think there might really be a place for me in the business!

After junior college I had the choice of either continuing on to Stanford or going to the world-famous Pasadena Playhouse. My dad had been against my becoming an actor but, fortunately, changed his mind after seeing me in a few shows. However, he added the stipulation that "If you're going to be an actor, you'd better be a good one." I hope I managed that and I know that in later years he became my biggest fan, so my choosing to go to the Playhouse seemed to work out well.

The Playhouse years were wonderful in many ways. The work we did was stimulating, difficult, and very rewarding. On the personal side, I also had my first affair, at age 20! That must have opened me up emotionally because I then proceeded to fall in love (with a different girl) for the first time—though not the last, I might add. She was a classmate from Chicago, was Jewish, I wasn't, her mother didn't approve, so, alas, that was that.

However, the concentrated work at school made me feel like I had chosen the right field. Getting a part in a play on Main Stage was everybody's goal, and I managed to do it in my senior year which was unheard of in those days. I played the juvenile lead in the Zoe Akins play called *Texas Nightingale*, which starred a lovely woman from Europe who did not speak English very well. Her name was Madame Leopoldine Konstantine and she was extremely talented and very sweet to me…until during one performance I wandered outside the stage door to get a breath of air and didn't get back in time for my cue. She was on stage and trying to ad-lib to cover for me but not succeeding very well because of her limited English! I forget which language she spoke, but whatever it was it was very colorful and I had no trouble knowing what she meant as she bawled me out for that gaffe, and rightly so. I never ever did that again in my whole career—a hard-learned lesson!

In my postgraduate year, I did a show in the prestigious PlayBox which Gilmor Brown, the founder of the school and theater, had developed in his large garage and backyard. It was there, while doing a show called *The Breath of Kings*, a bravura costume drama, that I was approached by talent scouts from Paramount, Warners, and Fox. In those days, the studios covered all the little theaters and theater schools looking for talent to put under contract, and I, of course, was delighted to be included!

One of my classmates was the beautiful Eleanor Parker who, as you will remember, went on to become a big movie star, and she and I talked over which studio we preferred, as she had been approached also. We decided on Warners and, borrowing a car from a classmate, went over to the studio together, were signed to make tests, and later made the tests, and were both signed to contracts on the same day! Making the test wasn't quite as easy as I've made it sound. I did a scene from a movie that Warners had just made called *The Corn is Green,* starring Bette Davis. Of course, I didn't get to work with *her* (I was just a contract player), but the material was wonderful and the cameraman was the famous James Wong Howe, one of the best in the business, so that was enough to get me a good case of "nerves"! I managed to control myself and completed the scene in good order. Good enough so they signed that wonderful contract with me...for $75 a week! What a thrill that was! Now that it was over, how easy it seemed.

How little I knew!

Chapter 3
The Warner Bros.Years

What a great thing to be under contract to a major studio! It doesn't happen anymore, but I got in on the last of the best years in Hollywood. Actually, it was like being in college in a sense because you were taking classes in addition to having the possibility of being cast in a real movie. I was given a sticker to put on the windshield of my car and had a dressing room on the lot, so I could drive up to the guard at the gate and be waved through, just as though I belonged there…which I did!

Incidentally, I say "my car." Well, on my fabulous salary of $75 a week I could afford to pay $85 for a very good used car, pay my monthly rent on a furnished apartment of $35 (and I had a roommate to share that), and could even buy some clothes. My very first tailor-made suit cost me $50! All this was in 1941, so things were a bit cheaper, as you can tell.

This was the time of the major movie moguls, and the studios controlled a contract player's life in all departments. That is, if you wanted to get that $75 a week. Even so, I guess I was luckier than most because I was cast in two major pictures immediately, and at the same time! That was possible because one of the pics was going up to Canada on location and the other was being done at the studio.

The first picture was *Captains of the Clouds* and a special train rolled out of Burbank, complete with banners on its side proclaiming the name of the picture and the stars. And what a cast it was: Jimmy Cagney, Dennis Morgan, Brenda Marshall, Alan Hale, Sr., Reginald Gardner, and George Tobias, all together. I had a "name" part and so rated a compartment, but my buddies who weren't so fortunate spend all five days on the train in my room where we played a lot of poker—one of the fellas was

15

Gig Young, before he became a star in his own right.

We arrived in Ottawa, Canada, and were put up at the Chateau Laurier, the finest hotel in town, from where we were driven each morning out to location, the airfield at Uplands. This was a film about the Royal Canadian Air Force, and, as it turned out, the student pilots who were in training there at that time were from all over the British Commonwealth and were the men who actually fought the Battle of Britain, the air war over London which defeated the Nazi Luftwaffe in the turning point of the air war.

Our director was a Hungarian gentleman named Michael Curtiz, who was rather tough on his actors, always calling them some kind of "bum." Most were called "Wednesday Bums" because Wednesday was pay day at the studio, but I got special attention. I was called a "Pasadena Bum" because Mike had found out that I had gone through the Pasadena Playhouse.

We were working in color, early color, so we needed a lot of light for the film. The very first shot I ever worked in on a picture was the master shot of the whole airfield with the actual regiment of trainees (all in the Canadian Air Force) lined up in parade formation with planes flying over in formation on cue. In the foreground, I was in the cockpit of a small training plane and was supposed to taxi up to a certain spot, stop, get out, take off my goggles and spread a map out on the wing of the plane. All of which sounds fairly simple except that it *was* my very first shot and it *was* with Jimmy Cagney, himself.

After we had set up the shot, a lot of clouds had come, obscuring the light, and Mike was wandering around muttering to himself in Hungarian because he couldn't shoot the scene, and it was holding up the whole war effort! You can imagine the state I was in after the rehearsal in the hot confines of the cockpit with Mike (for want of someone else to take his frustration out on), yelling at me to "get it right this time, you Pasadena Bum!" I could hardly see for all the "flop sweat" in my eyes! And, of course, just then the clouds parted and we were ready to shoot. It was a good thing that Jimmy had the first line!

On the call of "action," the planes flew over in perfect formation, and I managed to get my plane to the marked spot, get the canopy back, get my goggles off, get out of the plane, spread the map out on the wing (all in a daze), when Mr. Cagney walked up...and blew his line! As he did, he reached over, slapped me on the arm and said, "Don't let 'em getcha, kid!" It took me a few minutes to realize that he had blown the line on purpose because he had seen what had been happening to me. And, of course, Mike couldn't say anything to the biggest star on the Warner Bros. lot! The next time we did the scene, it went perfectly. What a fine gentleman that Mr. Cagney was, and I shall never forget what he did.

One other thing Mr. Cagney did for me in that picture was to change my name...in the pic, that is. My cast name was originally Lewis Prentiss, but Cagney objected that he couldn't say a name like that when he spoke to me, and then asked me if I could do a southern accent. When I replied that I could, I became "Alabama." I liked it a lot better, too.

After we had shot all the scenes at Uplands, a lot of the cast was going up North into the backwoods country to shoot up there. As I was playing a cadet, I didn't go and returned to the studio to wait for the company to get back to shoot other scenes of training on a soundstage. It was going to be a few weeks before they returned and, in the meantime, I was cast in my second picture. This was a very special one, too... *The Man Who Came to Dinner*! And, again, what a terrific cast I was going to work with!

Russ and Monty Wooley in *The Man Who Came to Dinner*, 1941.

Monty Wooley, Bette Davis, Liz Fraizer and Russ.

Here were Bette Davis, Monty Woolley, Ann Sheridan, Reginald Gardner, Billie Burke (remember her in *The Wizard of Oz* as the beautiful good witch?), and best of all, Jimmy Durante! I was in seventh heaven, and, of course, again terrified!

Another story I fondly remember concerns the wonderful Bette Davis. At that time she was one of the biggest stars at the studio, or in the picture business, for that matter. Well, the day I was to work for the first time, I reported to the assistant director to get my wardrobe okayed. I went to the big soundstage, and inside were dressing rooms, and the set on which they were shooting. The AD took me into the set and introduced me to the director, an English gentleman by the name of William Keighley. He was very cordial and said they would get to me a bit later, so not wanting to get in the way, I walked back out onto the soundstage and found a little chair way off in a corner.

I sat there in the semi-darkness waiting to be called when, suddenly, Bette Davis, herself, came walking out of the set and headed toward her dressing room. It happened to be in a different direction from where I was sitting, but she saw me out of the corner of her eye, stopped, and then headed in my direction! She approached me holding out her hand and said, "You're playing Richard, aren't you?" I immediately leapt to my feet and, trembling, took her hand and managed to get out the words, "Yes, Ma'am." To which she replied, "Well, we hope you have a good time," then turned on her heel and went off to her dressing room. I sat down very quickly before I could faint, wondering at the miracle that had happened! I know it doesn't sound like much, but to a "Pasadena Bum" it was something very special, indeed! I never forgot her kindness, just as I never forgot Jimmy Cagney's.

Billie Burke played my mother in the film and we had a scene with some dialogue in the living room, and then were to walk up some stairs while the scene continued below. We had to wait for a bit at the top of the stairs and we fell into conversation while they rehearsed the rest of the action. I reminisced about San Francisco, which was my hometown, and Miss Burke grew almost misty-eyed as she thought about that beautiful city. She then said that one of the things she hated about becoming a bit older was that she couldn't have someone take her to the top of the Mark Hopkins Hotel, have a sherry, and hold hands while looking out over the beautiful lights shining on the bay. Of course I eagerly volunteered to be the one to take her there, but, unfortunately, I never had the chance to do it. However, it was a lovely, romantic thought involving a lovely, romantic lady!

At the end of the shooting there was a "wrap" party at Mr. Keighley's house near the studio. It was held in the pool house which had a piano in it, which was fortunate because after the great Durante arrived, he took over and entertained us all afternoon. What a fabulous experience that whole picture was for me!

It wasn't long before the *Captains of the Clouds* company returned from Canada and was ready to shoot my scenes again, so I got out my uniform and prepared to work. At the end of the picture I was to be killed while training on a practice bombing run with Cagney as my instructor. That was fun...being killed, but I was glad it was only in a film! And, of course, that was the end of the picture for me. So now, instead of having two pictures going, I was left hoping to be cast again in something else. Gee, I thought: this Hollywood is a cinch! Little did I know!

My personal life was progressing, too. About this time a feisty, devil-may-care gal caught my attention. She was under contract and was doing a lot of parts, which was how I met her. As we were allowed to visit sets of various movies that were shooting, I spent a lot of time going from set to set to watch different directors and actors do their stuff. That was how Faye Emerson caught my eye. She later went on to become a big star in early TV as a talk show hostess but at this time she was just a hard-work-

Russ with Jimmy Cagney in *Captains of the Clouds*, 1941.

ing actress trying to get the "big break." I watched her and, finally, got up the nerve to speak to her…after all, I was under contract, too!

We got on well and one night at a party to which all us "kids" were invited, I ran into her again, only this time it was on a social basis, and, as luck would have it, she needed a ride home! Trying not to appear *too* eager, but with a pounding heart, I quickly volunteered to drive her, and that was the beginning of a beautiful friendship, as Bogie said in *Casablanca*!

Faye was fun and exciting to be with and for a year we had a wonderful romance until one sad day she came to me with a very serious face and told me it was over. She said she was too old for me (she was perhaps three years older) and she had to look out for her future, and, the funny thing was, I understood how she felt. So, that was the end of that, although we remained very good friends for years, until her untimely death. However, even after our official parting she used to come by my place in the wee small hours, roust me out of bed, and we'd sit and talk or whatever. Ah! My first Hollywood love!

That was 1941 and the draft was looming, but before I had to leave, I got another break by being cast in my third picture, *Wings for the Eagle*, which starred Dennis Morgan, Jack Carson, and Ann Sheridan. However,

Captains of the Clouds, 1941.

I did get fourth billing! It was about the war effort, more particularly about Lockheed making airplanes for the Air Force. I played a fella working at Lockheed alongside of Dennis until I joined the Air Force and, subsequently, got shot down in the Pacific. Of course, to make a good story, Dennis then had to join up and avenge me...which he did.

Again, I had a wonderful time on the picture and became great friends with Annie Sheridan. She even spent her spare time on the set knitting me a sweater to take along with me to the Army. I still have that sweater to this day! She also took some farewell publicity pics kissing me goodbye and they were run in the *L.A. Times* one day just before I left for basic training. What a nice thing that was to carry with me to show my bunkmates!

So, I was put on "suspension" with the promise that after the war I would return to my contact and continue my career. But who knew what changes there would be in the motion picture business by the time I got back…four years later! Unfortunately, I found out, the hard way, but even so, I was lucky to have had a contract to come back to. But before we get into all of that, let's talk about my Army career, which leads us right into the next chapter!

Chapter 4
You're In the Army Now

On my birthday, Feb. 3, 1941, I received my Greeting from Uncle Sam and had to report to the bus depot in downtown Los Angeles in exactly one week. Happy Birthday! On induction eve I called a young lady I had been seeing and asked if she would drive me downtown the next morning as I had to be there at 6:00 a.m. She must have really liked me because she was willing, and so it was that I became a citizen soldier. We were bussed to Fort MacArthur in San Pedro and, without further ado, did the necessary paperwork, were doled out uniforms, assigned bunks, and found ourselves lined up in a small room where we were told to strip, fold our stuff, and walk through a door at the end of the room.

Right here I should explain that I had been raised in the Christian Science religion, and so had never had any medicine or shots and thus was totally unprepared for what was to follow. The Army doesn't ask what your background is or what your preferences are, they're there to do a job—to make a soldier out of a civilian!

And so it was that, stark-naked and carrying my uniform in my arms, I stepped through that door and was assaulted by two medics, one on each arm. As we all did, I got a smallpox vaccination in my left shoulder and two shots in my right one: tetanus and typhoid! I then was told to dress and report for chow. It wasn't until about three hours later that it hit me. And I mean, HIT me! The upshot of it was that I passed out and wound up in the post hospital with a huge temperature!

Our unit was scheduled to leave via troop train in two days, so I had to get well enough to get on the train. I did manage to do that, but only because a new friend I had made at induction took care of me and explained to the second lieutenant who was in charge of getting us out of there what my problem was. He arranged to have one of the berths in the railroad car pulled down, and I was carried on board on a stretcher and put in the berth. I stayed there until we got to Camp Crowder in Neosho, Missouri, where I was immediately transferred to the post hospital. There I spend the next week out of my head. Some soldier!

I should explain that this was a new camp and so, to begin with, we were assigned "housekeeping" duties. That meant helping build roads and all kinds of good stuff like that. Of course we had all come in from Hollywood, and the cadre of regular Army troops, who were in charge of our unit, immediately decided we were all queer and they treated us accordingly.

One corporal took me on as his personal charge. He would go out and purposely get his boots muddy, stomp them in the barracks, and then make me clean his boots, as well as the muddy trail he had left. This kind of thing happened to all of us, and being brand-new recruits we didn't know enough to complain as we were constantly threatened with court-martial and other dire consequences if we refused "an order."

I had one other "advantage." My name began with "A" so I was always first on any kind of duty roster. That was fine, but it always worked out that some changes would occur before they got through the roster and they would then start all over again—with "A." So I had my share of KP, cleaning the latrines, and all the other things that made basic training such a joy. Oh, well!

I did get one break with KP and other chores, though. One day I was in fatigues, working hard, scrubbing out some huge pots, when an orderly tapped my sweaty shoulder and told me that a major wanted to see me at headquarters. This, of course, meant that I had to hurriedly clean myself up a bit, change into the proper uniform, and report . . . pronto! So, wondering what was going on, I managed to make myself presentable, got to the major's office, saluted smartly, and said the magic words, "Private Arms reporting as ordered, Sir." He immediately replied, "At ease," and then continued, "I understand, Arms, that you were an actor in Hollywood and that in your last picture you worked with Ann Sheridan."

When I heard these words, a little light went on in my head, a great weight lifted from my shoulders, and I really did become at ease as I replied, "Yes, sir, all of that is true." Then, with an ingratiating smile, he said, "Well, we are about to open a new post theater and wondered that if we called Miss Sheridan, who happens to be in the state on a USO tour, you would talk to her and see if you could get her to come here for an appearance. We will be able to get a copy of *Wings for the Eagle*, the picture that you and she were in, and thought it would be a great opening for the theater if the two of you were here." Feeling much better about my situation, I told him that I would be delighted to talk with Annie and see what I could do.

All of a sudden the major and I became buddies. He told me to sit down, got me a Coke, and proceeded to make the phone call. She was appearing at Ft. Leanord Wood, which is also in Missouri, but it took some time to get hold of her on the phone. They were using my name as bait, though I wasn't sure how tempting that would be to her.

Anyway, I was happy just sitting there drinking my Coke—much better than washing out those pots on KP—until, finally, she was on the phone and they handed it to me to talk with her.

She was absolutely wonderful, sweet as pie, and said she was more than willing to come, but couldn't as they had a schedule all planned out and she was leaving immediately for another base, which is just about what I expected she'd say. So, after more sympathy and love for me on the phone, we said our goodbyes and she asked to speak to the major again saying she'd give him the news, thus taking me off the hook.

After he accepted what she told him, the really good stuff began to happen. I guess they were so desperate to have something "special" at the opening of the new theater that they were willing to accept whatever they could get because he then asked me if I would make a solo appearance! I, of course, immediately agreed (no more KP) and plans were afoot for my big appearance. They did manage to get the picture *Wings for the Eagle* and I was in it. So, with all of that, I did become a small celebrity on the post.

I hasten to add, I wasn't a hero to my group 'cause they were all from Hollywood and were much bigger names in their fields that I was in mine. However, it worked out just fine for me, thanks to a nameless major and my beautiful Annie!

We finally finished our training, learning how to march, salute, etc. (all of which I knew because of those six years in military school). As our careers continued, I was offered several jobs, including that of medic, all of which I turned down. I had learned the old Army saying, "never volunteer" and kept to that sage advice.

Finally, and I really lucked out on this, we were assigned to various units and were shipped out. I had drawn the Signal Corps and was delighted because one of their responsibilities was, and is, to make training films, and that, of course, was one of the things that I knew something about. So I wound up at Ft. Monmouth, New Jersey.

This was the main post for the Signal Corps and encompassed all of the duties of the SC—including Long lines (stringing wires on telephone poles), radio operations, secret coding, phones for the office installations, and all the other things that one might expect of a signal organization. However, knowing that training films were part of the duties, I kept hoping and waiting for a permanent assignment.

Sure enough! One day orders came through for a number of us to report to the old Paramount Studios in Long Island City, N.Y. The Army had just taken over this installation and was making it the headquarters for all training film activity.

We were quartered in one of the soundstages where they had installed double-decker bunks, and we would fall out for reveille and the afternoon retreat ceremony in the city street. They made another of the stages into a mess hall and others became all the usual offices for official business, as well as for the unusual jobs of film editing, writers' rooms, etc., and of course kept some stages for their original purpose—the actual shooting of the films—all the paraphernalia of a film studio.

I was assigned to the casting office, of all places, but the name is misleading because we did a lot more than just cast training films. We were also in charge of all the narration that went into the films—the "how-tos": clean a rifle, read maps, dig a field latrine, and, of course, the "scare 'em" sex films that were supposed to keep the citizen soldier chaste and pure. What laughs!

Anyway, narration became one of my principal jobs, mainly because I could pick up a script and read it at sight as though I had written it. Which I often actually did! I sometimes felt that they wound me up at nine o'clock, stood me in front of a microphone, and turned me off at five o'clock! We often did secret films, so I had to be cleared for that category which, though extremely serious, was very exciting. I felt like I was playing in a spy picture, but this was for real. Incidentally, my file is littered with quite a number of commendations, so I guess my work was appreciated after all.

The Signal Corps Photographic Center very quickly grew into an important part of the war effort. It was found that film was an easy and effective way to train troops and so they used a LOT of it. As our installation grew, our living quarters were transferred to the old Capitol Hotel (now the

Lieutenant Arms, Signal Corps, 1945.

YWCA), near the original Madison Square Garden at 8th Avenue and 50th Street in Manhattan. They took over most of the floors, stripped them and installed standard issue beds, linen (believe me, they *weren't* linen), and all the equipment necessary to house several hundred men.

And, so, we became "Subway Commandos," as we had to ride the 8th Avenue subway out to Long Island City, but early, because we had to stand at reveille in the street at 7:00 a.m. every morning. But the best part of it was, they turned us loose after retreat in the evening and we were free until the next morning.

We may have been free, but we were broke! The going pay rate for a private was $21 per month, and that didn't go very far in New York even though all our housing and meals were provided for. So, we were always looking for any way to get some money.

My way was a bit strange, but it worked. My agent, Gus Dembling,

Dennis Morgan and Russ in *Wings for the Eagle*, 1942.

who I had signed with at the same time I had signed my contract with Warners, collected my fan mail from the studio and would ship it to me in a big box. I had decent parts in three pictures and, fortunately, had been noticed by the audiences which resulted in quite a bit of fan mail—and that thrilled me, I must say.

Anyway, in those days, when fans would write in for a picture they usually enclosed a quarter to pay for the pic, so when a big envelope or box would arrive for me, my buddies and I would gather around and go through the mail shaking every envelope for the telltale sound of the quarter inside. Unfortunately, not everyone enclosed their quarters, but enough did for me to collect several dollars which were a big help to my so-called finances! Things were a lot cheaper in those days and the few dollars I collected went a lot further than they would today.

I had never been in New York before but quickly got to know the town, mainly through my buddy, Frank Milan, who had been an actor in New York before the draft called. He still had many friends there which is why we got to spend many evenings in the posh clubs, like the Stork

Club, El Morocco, the Copa—all without a dime in our pockets! I really felt like a "rube"—"Hey, lookie at them tall buildings!"—that sort of thing.

Wartime New York was something else! People really tried to take care of the soldiers who were there on leave or were just there. Aside from all the fancy clubs, there was the Stage Door Canteen which did a yeoman's job of serving the service men. Many was the night that I didn't get to bed at all—or not in my own bed, at least. But I still had to make reveille and be able to function the next day. When you're young and healthy and in uniform…well, you do a lot of things you might not do at another time. The feeling that you are not in control of your own destiny makes you a bit irresponsible 'cause you don't' know what will happen tomorrow. Any day the "order" may come down and you're on your way. So, we enjoyed what we had while we had it!

Finally, an officer friend convinced me I should go to Officers Candidate School and become a lieutenant. It took some convincing, but I finally agreed and was very glad I did when it was all over. The four months I spent back at Ft. Monmouth becoming an officer were four of the hardest months I ever put in…to this day!

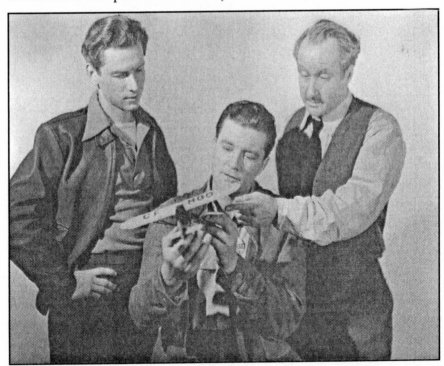

Dennis Morgan, Russ and George Tobias in *Wings for the Eagle*, 1942.

First, we took classes every day while being harassed by our tactical officers who were in charge of about 120 men all trying to "make it." Only about 70 actually did make it all the way through. The classes were extremely difficult as they leaned heavily on math (which I was, and still am, very bad at), map reading, engineering stuff, and a lot of other things that I managed to squeak through even though I really didn't comprehend a lot of it. I was very good at the military part though, again because of my military school experience.

In the fourth month, I was appointed regimental adjutant and among my many duties had to run the big graduation parade for all the brass. My acting really stood me in good stead here because I just played the part of a regimental adjutant, bawling out commands and putting the regiment through its paces. Actually, it was really exciting, and I was exhausted but very proud that it came off well.

And so I became a second lieutenant, an officer *and* a gentleman! Actually, that is about as low as you can get in the Army! On a small salary I had to provide for my uniforms, housing, and food. That salary didn't go very far, and I was delighted when some of my new friends in New York invited me to dinner, a party, or whatever.

I was returned to SCPC for a brief time before being shipped out to Camp McCoy, Wisconsin, for the final six months of my Army career. Just as I was being shipped out, the war in Europe ended and it looked like the Japanese part was pretty well under control, too.

While at Camp McCoy I had met the general's daughter, a very sweet girl, who was impressed that I had been an actor in Hollywood. That gave me a certain edge over other young officers about dating Ruthie, and soon, on occasion, the general sent his car around to the Bachelor Officers Quarters to pick me up. When that happened and the announcement went out over the loudspeakers that "the general's car is here for Lieutenant Arms," I wasn't the most popular chap in the barracks!

Thus, I became the "gofer" at parties in the general's house. I was the only junior-grade officer present, of course, so I made myself available for any, and all, chores. Anything to keep the general happy! But I did enjoy myself, too, because the thing the general liked to do the most was to gather folks around the piano and sing! Talk about breaks, 'cause I did know something about that! I have to say, though, that these were genuinely nice people, and I was lucky to have the opportunity to be a part of their lives.

Russ and Ann Sheridan on the Warner Bros. lot, 1942.

One sidebar to the McCoy experience. I was issued a Jeep and a WAC photographer (well, I wasn't issued the WAC!) because one of my duties, by then, was to pick up the photographer and be at any function the general attended to make sure that proper pictures were taken of the event. As he attended a lot of functions that meant I got to know the good-looking photographer quite well. And so it came about that in the cold and the snow (it was December in Wisconsin) I would get in my little Jeep and drive over to the dark room where my WAC was developing the day's shoot and would assist her in any way I could. It was nice and warm in that little shack, and so one thing led to another, and...well, you know! Who said life in the Army wasn't tough!

Finally the day came when I had enough points to get out of the service. A very complicated point system had been set up to make one eligible

Sergeant Arms, 1943.

for release, and, at last, my numbers added up, mainly because, by this time, I had been in service for four years. I really felt it was time to go back to Warners where my contract had another year and a half to run. It took some doing at that, because the general had taken a liking to me and wanted me to stay in and make the service my career. In addition, while being discharged, they offered me a captaincy if I'd sign on for another hitch.

But, in spite of all the blandishments, I desperately wanted to go back to California and the studio and to resume my acting career. Little did I realize that things had changed drastically out there. If I had known a bit more about the realities of Hollywood in the postwar years, I might have taken a little more time before returning. But I really did want to be a civilian again, and so, almost four years to the day that I was drafted, I was discharged. Not a thrilling career, but it took four years out of my life, and I did contribute something to the war effort. I must say that I was very proud of a few things I did…and maybe not so proud (ha!) of a few other things! You know, young and healthy and in wartime New York City…*well!*

There is a psychological effect to being in uniform because with so many people wearing the same color and same clothing one tends to fade into obscurity, or to become "faceless." You have to think hard about your behavior under those circumstances. At least that's the way it is in wartime, and that may help explain some of the strange things which occurred during that period. I'm very grateful that I escaped anything really drastic while I was in uniform. And I did learn a lot about life!

Chapter 5
The Warner Bros. Redux

Although it was wonderful to be a civilian again, it took some doing to adjust to my new life. Fortunately, I still had my contract at Warners and my salary was up to $150 a week, which was good because many things had changed in the four years I had been away. For instance, there was no housing to be had, and I had to bunk in with friends until I could locate an apartment, or even a room. I did manage to buy back my car from the friend who had bought it from me when I left for the Army, so transportation was no problem, but finding a place to stay was nigh impossible. I finally found a little house that had a back room with a private entrance and, with not much choice, took it.

The studio was different, too. With everyone coming back from service and fewer markets for their product, the studios were having a hard time of it and were all beginning the process of letting people go in every department, even those who had been employed for many years. I knew I was guaranteed at least a year (it lasted a year and a half, actually) of employment, and so I wasn't too concerned about paying the bills, but I was very concerned about finding parts with which to resume my acting career. The old adage of "out of sight, out of mind" certainly applied here; nothing was forthcoming except small bits in some small movies. You had to look quickly to see me at all and, as I was under contract to the studio, I couldn't look for work elsewhere, so I was kind of stuck.

However, one very nice thing did happen. There was to be a preview showing of a big picture at the Warner Theatre in Hollywood, with all the hoopla that used to accompany an opening in those days. The publicity department called and asked if I would escort a new contract player to the premiere. I was reluctant to agree until they told me it was Arlene Dahl! With that, my attitude changed entirely, and I was more than delighted to accede to their wishes. I probably would never have had the nerve to ask her myself, her beauty was so stunning that I wouldn't have been able to get the words out, and here they were asking me to do *them* a favor!

Fortunately, it turned out well. She was every bit as nice inside as she was outside, and the evening, complete with klieg lights, interviews, and a mob of fans shouting and flashing their cameras, was great fun. But, best of all, we hit it off personally very well and I was able to see a good deal more of Arlene in the ensuing months. We became an "item" as they used to say in the papers.

Jack L. Warner, who ran the studio, had been in the Army briefly, came out a lieutenant colonel, so everyone at the studio called him "Colonel." He loved to play tennis and was always looking for playing partners. One day I received a phone call from the casting office and was asked if I played tennis. When I said that I did, I was invited up to Jack's house the following Sunday morning to play. Getting all dressed up in my "whites," I showed up at the appointed time, not at the gorgeous, big house itself, but at the little house down by the tennis court. (I have never seen the actual big house to this day!)

Finally, the great man appeared, along with several other players, and we began playing doubles. There were a lot of shouts of "Good shot, Colonel," and that type of thing, which were uncalled for, I might add, for although Jack loved the game, he was, to say the least, a middling player. I stood it as long as I could and then, as he hit a ball completely over the fence, which was around the court, I shouted out, "Good shot, Colonel!" The sycophants' faces turned gray and a quiet had settled over the court, but we continued to play. Need I add that I was never asked back to play tennis at Mr. Warner's house again?! I knew that my contract was going to be up soon, so what did I have to lose? I was undoubtedly an idiot but I just couldn't help myself.

Another thing Jack was famous for was his walking around the studio lot and checking the lights on the soundstages. He had several people who trotted along behind him and, if they were told, would turn out the lights if they weren't being used. Not a bad idea—but the head of the studio?!

Anyway, one day I had just been watching them shoot some picture and was standing on a street corner getting a breath of fresh air when along came Jack and his toadies. Seeing me standing there, he suddenly whirled and demanded, "Who are you and what are you doing here?" I couldn't believe he was addressing me, but he sure was! Quickly I stammered that I was an actor under contract to the studio and was studying my craft or some such smart remark. He looked at me in disbelief, as if to say, "Do I actually have such an idiot under contract to my studio?" Well, that's the way he made me feel, and, with that, he turned on his heel and went on with his light-turning-out. That was the only time I ever spoke with Jack Warner face-to-face at the studio. Of course he may have remembered me from the tennis game, but I doubt it!

However, I must say that I LOVED the time I was under contract to the studio. It gave me a big boost up when I was just starting in the business, and I got to know a lot of wonderful people in the process. Of course the time came when they dropped my contract and I was, as they say, "at liberty," which simply means I needed a job!

Casting about in my mind as to what I could do, I remembered my bunkmate from the very early days as SCPC in the Army. His father had produced the famous Hopalong Cassidy series of westerns, and Jerry Thomas, my "bunkie," was producing two series on his own, both quickie Westerns. One was with Lash LaRue, and the other was with Eddie Dean. Now those of you in the major metropolitan areas may not know of these two gentlemen, but if you are from the South or Southwest, or even the Midwest, you surely remember them. Their series were both very successful, and when I told my bunkie that I needed a job, Jerry, without a moment's hesitation, replied "come on over," and he put me to work. Bless him for that!

I wound up doing several episodes of each of the series and had a wonderful time playing "cowboys and Indians." Fortunately, I could ride very well from having rented horses in my youth and riding in the hills above Burlingame. Good thing because I had to do all my own riding in the pics, though not the stunts. These pictures were shot very quickly, usually in three days, so it was a whole different world, and, again, I met some wonderful people who taught me a lot about the "western world." I played bad guys, young heroes, or just about anything that Jerry thought I was physically right for. Thanks, Jerry!

Later on, I was called by Columbia studios to do another Western film, this with Roy Acuff, who was better known on the Grand Ol' Opry radio and TV shows than in movies. This time I played a young hero,

Russ interviewing Janis Paige and Joyce Reynolds in *Wallflower*, Warner Bros., 1948.

actually a young punk, but he became the hero, finally, after Roy straightened him out! I played the same character, but with a different name and in another film, this time with Gene Autry.

On the strength of these films and the other ones I had done for Jerry Thomas, Columbia offered me a contract to do Westerns. And on the second pic I did with Gene Autry, he asked me if I had ever considered making a career of being a movie cowboy! I didn't know it at the time, but he owned a TV property called *The Range Rider* and was feeling me out about playing the lead in it. Like a dummy, I told Gene that I didn't want to be a cowboy actor much longer, that I was planning on going back to New York and trying the stage, which had been my main ambition from the very beginning.

Anyway, the fella who got the part was much more qualified for it than I was. His name was Jock Mahoney, and he was the best man on a horse that I had ever seen. He had doubled for me in one of the Autry pictures, *Loaded Pistols*, and had taught me some of the fancy mounts and dismounts that he was so great at doing. He was a wonderful man, who went on with two successful TV series and a success he greatly deserved.

So, still dreaming great dreams about the New York stage, I was more than ready when a buddy of mine, Craig Stevens (who later went on to become Peter Gunn on TV), called and asked me to drive to New York with him. A buddy of his, John Horton, was going back into the Army as a lieutenant colonel to be on President Truman's White House staff, an exciting prospect! We three would drive to Washington, drop John off, and then Craig and I would continue on to New York and pursue our careers. The trip had a lot of possibilities and so, without further ado, off we went.

Two things I remember about the trip itself: feeding the chipmunks on the Continental Divide and driving through the city of Craig, Colorado, where we photographed Craig leaning on a garbage can which had "Keep Craig Clean" stenciled on its side. Well, we thought it was hilarious at the time!

Arriving in Washington, we were put up by some friends of John's and had three days of Washington glamour—went to see the house of our first president and had the thought that the people of that time were very small, or so the rooms in the house would make you think. But it was a beautiful place and we enjoyed it. We also enjoyed meeting the current president, Mr. Truman, along with his daughter, Margaret. It was very impressive to be right there in the middle of things, and I have to admit that I was completely awestruck!

And, speaking of awestruck…if you ever have the chance to see the Lincoln Memorial in person, run, do not walk, to do so! It is a hallowed place and one that I guarantee will affect you emotionally. I admit that I stood with tears running down my face as I looked at the statue of that great man!

We also went to a couple of parties hosted by Army buddies of John, so our trip started out very well. But, too soon, we drove off to see what lay ahead in New York.

Housing was kind of hard to come by, but we managed to find a four-flight walk-up on 49th Street just off Broadway. I must say that, although convenient to Times Square, this wasn't the most ideal spot to live in the city mainly because of the several restaurants on that street. Each morning about 4:00 a.m. the garbage trucks would line up to collect garbage from each and every one of them and I can't begin to describe the racket they made! With nothing to be done about it, we buried our heads in our pillows and waited for the din to subside. We did get a bit used to

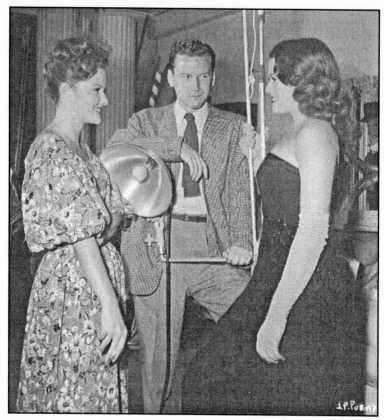

A pause between takes with Martha Vickers (left) and Janis Paige on the Warner Bros. lot.

it after a couple of weeks, and, so, with that first problem out of the way, we set about finding agents who would help us to find work.

In order to pay the rent, I immediately called out to my old stomping ground, the Signal Corps Photographic Center. This time, instead of casting the films, I was asking to be cast in them. Fortunately, some of my old friends were still out there, this time as civilians, but they did give me several jobs. I was very grateful for that because it enabled me to stay in New York for a while longer. I had gotten an agent—the New York office of my Hollywood agent, General Artists Corp.—and they were very interested in trying to find me work.

And so, the next chapter will be New York Redux and the time I would be a civilian in the great city!

Chapter 6
Acting Is Fun

I want to digress just a bit before going on with my New York adventures. Looking backwards over my life I feel that I've been fortunate in my career for many reasons. First, I've had a lot of jobs in many venues: radio, movies, the legitimate stage, outdoor shows, rodeos (yes!), fashion shows, emcee work for pageants, narration for commercials and industrial films— just name it and I've probably done it! So, when you have been so many places and done so many things, you naturally meet a lot of different people. What I'm getting at is you have to learn how to deal with all those different personalities and egos.

Most people feel that acting is easy—fun, glamorous, exciting. In a movie they make you up, tell you where to stand, and you say a few words in a short scene with some beautiful people and that's all there is to it. How many times have you said to yourself, "Why, I could do THAT!" Well, I suppose that's how Hollywood would like you to think about it, but let me fill you in a bit about, as Paul Harvey would say, the REST of the story.

Once I was cast in a play, to co-star Jane Wyatt, and the plot had me chasing after the ingénue who was being played by a young New York actress coming out to California for her first time. (It turned out that she actually did become a well-known movie actress later on). However, in our stage show, she was just starting out. All well and good, except when we came to the intimate scenes, where I had to kiss and hold her close (and anything else I could get a hold of!), it turned out that she had a terrible, all-encompassing body odor, so bad that I could barely breathe and certainly couldn't think of kissing and hugging and all that good stuff.

41

So, I was rather lukewarm in my pursuit, to the consternation of the director. He took me aside and chewed me out a bit until I told him my reason—that I couldn't breathe. Then he had to admit that he, too, had noticed the BO and went on to suggest that I tell her about it! "ME," I screamed, "No, No, No...YOU do it, you're the director!" Well, he wouldn't, of course, but he did tell her boyfriend (how could HE stand it?), who told her and she, in turn, told me...boy, did she ever! I was so upset, though, that I just lectured her on social hygiene and common courtesy to fellow actors and the like, which she didn't get.

One of my chores in the play was to pick her up and drive her to rehearsals as she lived near me. However, the next day when I went to get her, she was late. I waited until she came running out of the house, dripping from the armpits, and screaming at me, "I am late because I was WASHING!" Well, I couldn't complain about that, could I?

Incidentally, they had bought her a beautiful designer gown to wear in the play and by the time it was over it had become a beautiful designer RAG. To each his (her) own!

Another short story about disappointment concerns a different play and another unknown leading lady. We were in rehearsals when she walked in at the far end of the room. My eyes lit up immediately because from a distance she looked lovely and had a great figure and walk. But, alas, as she got closer, the flaw appeared. Her face, though pretty, was covered with zits (nay, pustules), whiteheads, yesterday's makeup, and just plain dirt! This time I swallowed hard and didn't say anything. Just did my best, but I did as little kissing as possible!

However, there are some good stories, too, I'm happy to say. For instance, did you know that I was the first Hollywood leading man for Zsa Zsa Gabor? True! I was under contract to Warner Bros. when they decided to make a test of the beautiful Hungarian. The casting office called me and asked if I would do the test with her and, of course, I said "yes" for a couple of reasons. When you were under contract, they had a miserable thing in the contract called "layoff." This meant that if you weren't actually working in a picture during a six-month period they could "lay you off" for six weeks, meaning without pay. However, if the studio called you in for any reason whatsoever they had to pay you for the whole week. So, as I wasn't working at the moment, I was happy to avoid "layoff" and get my week's pay or, in this case, three weeks pay because of the rehearsal time! And, of course, the other reason was the lady herself.

Russ and Virginia Christie in *Cover Up*, an independent film.

Zsa Zsa Gabor was brand new in town, along with her whole beautiful family, and was anxious to get started in the movie business, so she was happy to be making the test. I had never actually met her, but was delighted when I finally did. She was dazzling to be around, constantly chattering and looking gorgeous, never a dull moment.

So they gave her a scene for us to work on for the test and we started rehearsing. The actual test was scheduled for a couple of weeks later, so we had plenty of time. I would go up to the house ready to work, but with all the Gabors, inside it sounded like a Hungarian aviary and so we didn't get too much done. When we did work, though, everyone became kibitzers with many suggestions about the dialogue, scene, interpretation, or what to have for dinner for all I know, because they spoke mostly in Hungarian. So

I just sat and smiled and enjoyed myself. After all, I already had a contract!

We spent a lot of time lying on the carpet in front of the fireplace going over lines—and that's all we went over!—until the time came to actually shoot the test. So, the test was made, the studio didn't sign her, and that's the last I ever saw of Zsa Zsa. I did read about her a whole lot, though! And I did meet her beautiful sister, Eva, again later on, so it wasn't a total loss. I only wish I had learned to speak Hungarian!

Right after the war when things were very slow at the studio, I had an offer to do a play in downtown Los Angeles at the Mayan Theater. The studio said they would put me on the dreaded "lay off" and allow me to do the show, so off I went. I knew immediately that the play wasn't much, but all I wanted was to work and there were no films forthcoming that I could see, so I signed on.

The play was called *The Turquoise Matrix* and I was to play a young Indian chap clad in breechclouts who was in love with a lissome young thing and had to deal with all the usual folderol that went with that. Also in the cast was the usual priest in robes giving fatherly advice, etc. You get the picture, I'm sure. I have no idea why anyone in their right mind would want to mount this turkey.

In charge of the whole affair was a young tyrant who had been a stage manager in New York and was now moving up to being a director. Also, we only had a week to rehearse before we opened! So you can see the state of mind I was in! And why, you may ask, would I want to be in this thing? Well, actors are funny—they are totally insecure and are really nothing unless they are working. You always have the feeling after you close in a show or picture that you will never work again; ask any actor and he'll tell you the same thing.

So, off we went with the director breathing down our necks and everyone trying to memorize lines with opening night getting closer all the time. And it finally arrived! Wonder of wonders, we actually had a good-sized audience, though not for long!

The opening of the second act was me and the priest on a bare stage—and he had the first line! Well, there's an old saying in the theatre: "the curtain went up and he went up with it," which is exactly what happened to the good Father. So, there I stood in my skivvies wondering what to do or say as he stood absolutely frozen to his spot until I managed to throw enough semi-lines at him for him to come to and get on with it. Which was typical of how the whole show went.

So we opened and closed on the same night. What else was left to do, but take my leading lady home with me to spend the night, comforting each other's bruised egos. We had worked very hard and it had all come to naught, but, I must admit, it wasn't totally unexpected!

However, the topper to the whole thing came recently at a party here in Palm Springs. Someone I had just met reached into her handbag and came out with a program to, you guessed it, *The Turquoise Matrix*! After all those years, and I didn't even keep one of those myself!

I've always felt that the shining blonde singer-actress, Marvel Maxwell, better known as Marilyn Maxwell, or even better known to her friends as "Max," was responsible for my becoming a singer. We had met at the Pasadena Playhouse and become good friends and, in the course of an occasional date, found ourselves dancing one evening to the Tommy Dorsey Orchestra then playing at the Hollywood Palladium. Max had been a band singer and knew most of the big band folks, so between sets we were able to go backstage where she introduced me to the players and singers, notably Frank Sinatra, who was then with the band. What a thrill that was!

As the evening wore on and while we were dancing, I sang in her ear a bit, as one is wont to do, until she pulled back and said, "You should be a singer. You have a beautiful voice." A few years later that remark came back to me and gave me the courage to say "yes" when my agent asked me if I could sing. So I did an audition for my own radio show, got the job, and, thus, launched my singing career. Thank you, Max!

Here's a little story about Max that I probably shouldn't tell, but I will. Right after the war it was difficult to find a place to live so I was staying with my friend, John Alvin, in his house in Woodland Hills. It was on the side of a hill, with a long, winding road leading up to it—this was important as you shall see.

Max and I had been dating for a while and so were very close, to the point that I felt it was about time for me to make the pitch, you know, "the pitch." So I lured her out to John's house, which was the only place I had to go, and proceeded to lure away in my most charming manner. Everything was going very well and I was just about to take her by the hand and lead her to the bedroom, which she seemed more than willing to do, when I heard John's car on that long, winding road leading to the house! So we quickly had to shevel our disheveled selves and forget the whole thing! Rats! Somehow, I never got another chance to make a "pitch" with her!

However, I thoroughly enjoyed being around Max as she had the facility to put everyone at ease and make things relaxed and happy, but the best part of all was that she was a wonderful kisser! She passed away much too soon.

Well, enough digression, so let's get on with a more detailed account of my storied career—Ha! I think I was luckier than most, though, and we'll find out how lucky when we go back to New York where the fun really began because, as I said earlier, acting (and singing) is Fun!

Chapter 7

New York Redux

Being a civilian in New York was a whole lot different from being there in the Army! This time I had to provide for everything myself, but, somehow, I knew it would all turn out okay.

We stayed in that 49th Street apartment until Craig decided he would go back to Hollywood, and it was a good choice because it wasn't too long before he got his *Peter Gunn* television series which made him a star. But I was wondering what to do when my agent came up with a solution. His mother had an apartment on 52nd Street, just off Lexington, and was leaving it, so I could sublet it. I was delighted, of course, especially as the rent was $65 a month! I had to share a bathroom with the front apartment, but that made no difference to me. It was a one-flight walk-up compared to the four flights I had before, so that was a great improvement already.

My agent had an idea about putting a show together using a number of his clients and then inviting some directors, producers, casting agents, and whoever else might be helpful, to come see it. It was kind of like a backers' audition but with the talent on display rather than the script—an exciting idea, and I was anxious to jump in wherever I could, which turned out to be in four of the eight scenes.

During the rehearsals I made a number of new friends, of course, and when another friend, who had gotten a job in a show that was trying-out in Manhattan rather than on the road, called and asked if I wanted a couple of tickets to a preview, I jumped at the chance. I didn't know too many people in town yet, but I was working with an attractive girl in one of the scenes, so I asked her if she'd like to go with me to the preview. She said she'd love to, so with my free tickets I was all set.

All went well as I picked her up and we went to the theater. The seats were wonderful, fourth row center, and we (or I, I guess) settled down to enjoy the show. However, about the middle of the first act, I suddenly felt her hand groping my crotch! Ordinarily, in another place, I wouldn't have minded so much, but in a brightly lit theater it was a bit unnerving! Fortunately, it was wintertime and I had my overcoat with me, so I quickly adjusted it and whispered that we should wait until after the show. Nothing doing! She was eager and ready to have some fun. Finally, the intermission came and we quickly got up and moved to the back of the theater, where it was darker. I suggested we go home, but she wanted to stay and see the rest of the show—yikes! So we sat back down and resumed watching, but it wasn't long before she was up to her old tricks. I really sweat it out for the rest of the show, especially because standing not far behind us were some of the production people, and I do believe they were noticing the peculiar goings-on. I know I was, and not enjoying it! But, finally, finally, the show was over! Now we could go home and continue what she had started…or so I thought.

We did go to my apartment where she told me she had a date to keep at 1:00 a.m., but would come back after that. Okay, I said, but what about a drink now? Well, she didn't want a drink but I could go ahead if I liked, so I went into the kitchen to mix myself a vodka and tonic when she came strolling in smoking a joint…marijuana! I had never come into contact with dope of any kind and this was really a shock to my naiveté. But she wasn't through yet! I refused a drag, so she went back into the living room as I finished mixing my drink. When I went back into the living room she was standing at the mantel busily working on some white powder and asked for a razor blade to chop it up. I didn't even know what it was! You have to remember that I didn't even have an affair until I was 20, so I suppose I was somewhat retarded. When I finally realized that she was messing with COCAINE, I about fainted! So, she sniffed it and I hurriedly tried to get my drink down so I could get her out of there. But, no, my troubles were just beginning.

Soon she began to feel the effects, so off came her clothes, and she began advancing on me. All I could think about was someone bursting into the room and that would be the end of my career, and it hadn't even started yet! She was also beginning to be a bit loud, which made it even worse. I KNEW someone would come busting in, but all it took to calm her was to react to her sexual advances a bit which I grudgingly admit I did—just to quiet her down, you understand! So when it was over, I quickly reminded her that she had a date at one o'clock. With that, she got dressed and promised she'd be back as soon as she could. I told her I had an early rehearsal and not to come back, but at about four o'clock there she was, standing out in the hallway and hollering my name while pounding on the door!

Of course I had to let her in before the cops arrived, so I opened the door. I don't know what she had been doing (though I can guess), but she was a bit quieter. I made her sleep on the couch while I took the bed, and I was gone before she got up the next morning. I hoped that would be the end of it, but for about a month she would call three or four times a week with each call coming in the wee small hours of the morning. She would be at a party, and bombed, and would talk dirty to me until I'd hang up, telling her not to call me anymore. What an experience...and my introduction to civilian New York!

In the meantime, we had done that show for the agent, and some good had come from it. I had an interview for a Broadway show, two callbacks, and then didn't get the part. But it was a start. One day he called and asked me if I could sing. In this business you never say no, so I said, "sure." I also remember the beautiful Marilyn Maxwell, who had been a band singer and whom I dated at one time, pulling back from my shoulder as we were dancing, as I was crooning in her ear, saying to me, "Hey, Russ, you should be a singer! You have a beautiful voice!" So, remembering this, I had the nerve to say to the agent that, of course, I could sing. Thus, on the next Friday afternoon, I went up to WNEW, the biggest of the New York independent radio stations, to do an audition for a show— what kind, I didn't know or care. Maybe it was a job!

I had never sung professionally before but had hired a piano player (for $10) to accompany my audition, and, with two pieces of sheet music in my hand, walked into the station. I was met by a very nice gentleman who promptly told me to go into a studio and ad lib him a 15-minute show. I gasped and asked him what kind of show, but he said he didn't care, just anything I wanted to do. Well, when you're young and eager, you're capable of trying just about anything.

So into the studio we went and, thinking madly, I started. I managed to work in two songs ("It's Magic" was one of them, as I recall) and to even fake a commercial, when I looked up into the booth and he was signaling me to sign off. I recognized the sign of a slice across the throat, so I signed off and he waved to me to follow him.

Russ's radio show on WNEW-NY, 1948.

We went into the station manager's office to see him sitting with his feet on his desk and smoking a big cigar. He had been listening to me, of course, and without further ado he said, "Well, I'll tell you what I'll do...you start your own show on Monday..." (Remember this was Friday afternoon.) "You'll be on for 15 minutes at four in the afternoon, five days a week. I'll give you a writer/producer to work with you and you furnish the music! The pay is $45 per week!" (Remember this was 1948!) All in a whirl, I gasped out that that would be fine. That's how the Russ Arms Show was born, and how I became a professional singer!

I staggered out into the hall, wondering how I was going to have any music by Monday, when the girl singer at the station, who had been lurking in the hallway waiting for the results of the audition, ran up to me and asked if I was going to be with them. Still a bit dizzy from what had just happened, I said that I guessed I was. And then, bless her heart, she asked me if I had any music, and upon hearing my negative reply she invited me to come home with her and borrow some of her arrangements until I could get some of my own! Which I did for the first month of the show.

As we started down the hall to leave the building, a studio door suddenly opened and I was dragged inside to find myself in the middle of a musical show being done at the moment. When I looked up, the announcer was introducing me over the air as the new singer on the station and telling everyone to be sure and listen each day at four o'clock to hear me. Then he asked me to sing a song "just as a sample of what they had to look forward to!" Well, why not! The bandleader turned out to be a wonderful guy and asked me what song I wanted to do. I answered the first thing that came into my mind, which turned out to be "I'm in the Mood for Love," and then he asked, "What key?" I said, "I dunno, just pick one that might be appropriate," and, without batting an eye, he did, and then I did, and that was the first professional song I ever sang...and it turned out all right! Talk about being tossed in the pool and told to swim!

Apropos of all this is what I have always told young hopefuls when they ask me about getting a job in show business. You never know when an opportunity will come along unexpectedly and you must be prepared for it when it does come along. Once you get that foot in the door you must be able to deliver, and this means many long hours of lessons, rehearsals of particular songs, singing at every opportunity: in church, your living room, a party, anywhere you can sing in front of people. That's the key to help you get over your nerves and be able to concentrate on your performance. It's very important to work in front of people.

So, on Monday, I started my show on schedule, and it continued for 26 weeks. In the middle of the run the agent called me again and told me to get right over to the Dumont Theater on 7th Avenue. (As I remember, this was the theater from which Jackie Gleason did his famous *Honeymooners* show). They were looking for a "boy singer" to replace one who was leaving. So, off I went. Arriving at the theater, I was walking down an aisle toward the stage when I noticed a small group of people sitting in the audience.

One of them looked familiar and turned out to be a guy I had been in the Army with and who was now the director of this show! As our eyes met he gave the "okay" sign, and I knew I had the job even before auditioning—and that's the way it turned out. So now I had two jobs at once—a radio show and a TV show—and I was happily accepting the situation as normal!

The TV show was called *School Days* and was a spin-off of an old Gus Edwards vaudeville show. Our emcee, or teacher, was Kenny Delmar, the Senator Claghorn from the old Fred Allen radio show, so he was familiar, and one of the "students" was Buddy Hackett, the great comic. Buddy was just getting his start and during the run of the show we became good friends. He used to come over to my apartment and, just by talking, would have me in stitches, just a naturally funny guy. The other kids in the show were youngsters trying to get a start in the business, just as I was.

This happy combination of events went on for nine weeks before it inevitably came to an end. Now I was without a job at all after having had two at once, a normal situation, indeed! But I'm convinced that an angel sat on my shoulder looking out for me because very shortly thereafter, my agent called again and told me to get over to CBS. But that's the next chapter in the book. So, please turn the page!

Chapter 8

Early Live TV In New York

Television was really just getting started in 1948 and New York was the place to be if you wanted to be involved. I guess I was just in the right place at the right time because I seemed to be able to go from one show to another. My ubiquitous agent called and told me to go to CBS to audition for a brand-new show that was an hour in length and would have all original music. It would be called *The 54th Street Revue* because it was to be done in the 54th Street Theater—makes sense! (This theater later became the one where the Ed Sullivan show was produced and had its name changed to The Ed Sullivan Theater. And, of course, it's now where the *David Letterman Show* is produced.)

Well, I went in for my interview, which consisted of singing a song and reading some lines, both of which I did. For some reason I felt "off" and thought I had done a really lousy audition, and that feeling was strengthened when they gave me a cold goodbye and showed me the door. Actors are always so insecure! Even if you close in a show that was a big hit, you somehow have the feeling that you will never work again. It comes from doing auditions, I guess, having to prove yourself over and over again!

Anyway, I went back to my apartment, really angry with myself, began cursing and kicking things, and had just poured myself a drink when the phone rang. It was my agent, telling me they wanted me to be on the show! I couldn't believe it, but the offer was true and, best of all, the salary was to be $125 a week.

After I caught my breath, I nonchalantly said that would be fine and I'd take the job after which I hung up and collapsed! I wound up staying over a year with that show and learned a lot in the process.

Russ with Virginia Gibson and Carl Reiner (in chef's hat) in *54th Street Revue*, 1948.

This was the time of LIVE TV, no tapes or film, just the show, and it had to be done right the first time 'cause you didn't get a second chance. I went over to the theater about a week later for the first rehearsal and to meet my fellow cast members. Nice people. To begin, our master of ceremonies was a very nice guy named Jack Sterling. He was a big star on radio in New York and was now moving over to TV.

The show consisted of sketches and songs mostly, so the cast had to be able to sing, dance, read lines, and do comedy sketches. Our leading lady was Joan Diener, who starred in *Kismet* on Broadway later on, but like the rest of us, was just getting her start at this time. A little note about Joan—she was amply, well, shall we say doubly—amply endowed in the bosom department and had the tendency to wear low-cut dresses. Guess she figured if you got it, flaunt it! Well, the producer went her one better—he always brought a flower of some kind and stuck it in her cleavage to make sure we didn't get taken off the air! I must admit that it did look pretty and one could look without being obvious, just admiring the flower! I did enjoy admiring those flowers very much!

Another cast member was Carl Reiner, the comedian, writer, and, later on, actor and producer of several very successful TV series, including being in that great comedy cast on the Sid Caesar show. And, not to forget, he is the father of Rob Reiner who went on to become a big TV star, and is now a successful director. But this was Carl just getting his start, too.

The show was fun to do, and a lot of work because we had to learn all original music each week. I usually did two or three numbers, sometimes with a girl to sing to or dance with, and always two or three comedy sketches. It was an hour-long show, so there was a lot to do. One of the writers on the show, both script and music, was a man named Ted Fetter who became a good friend and would affect my life and career in a big way, but I'm getting ahead of myself.

In the Christmas season of 1948 I did an acting job on a Christmas show for NBC. Swathed in big Arab robes, complete with a hood, I played a messenger to the king. Wasn't much of a role, but it was a job, and I had to pay the rent. It happened that on the show was a young lady who was to sing "Ave Maria" and it turned out that she was from California, just as I was. So, with that opening, I made a lot of conversation and got her phone number.

She was staying at the Barbizon Hotel, a famous for-women-only place where the young ladies could escape the advances of the big city wolves, who were out there in packs. At least that's the way they made you feel—no gentlemen above the second floor, etc. You get the picture, I'm sure! Well, after the show that night I called to wish her a Merry Christmas. She wasn't in, but I left a message and waited for a couple of days to call her again. When I finally did reach her, she told me she was very impressed that I had remembered to call, and that gave me further courage, so I asked her out.

Lovejean Weber was her name and she had been in some sort of show business from her babyhood. Her father was a singer in vaudeville and one night during his act she had wandered on stage. As she was a very cute four-year-old, she was an immediate hit, so they kept it in the act. With her mother playing piano for her father, it became a neat little family act, and they traveled around working in all parts of the country. Unfortunately, however, during one of the trips they were in a bad automobile accident and her father was killed. After that, her mom played for silent pictures and Lovejean took dancing and singing lessons and got very good at it.

So good, in fact, that she had an audition at Universal Pictures and they signed her to become one of the "Jivin' Jacks and Jills" in the Donald O'Connor pictures that were such big hits at that time. She also did a lot of club dates and any kind of show that would hire her, and so it was that she was in New York for the Christmas show where we met.

We dated a lot and fell in love. Just about the time we decided to get married (I was 29 and this was the first time I had wanted to get married), she had an audition to be a replacement in the Broadway show, *Inside USA*, which starred Jack Haley and Bea Lillie. They were going to stay another month on Broadway and then go out on the road for about six weeks, which gave us time to plan for the wedding and decide what we wanted to do later on. What we wanted to do, of course, was to both have careers in show business—Broadway, TV, movies, or whatever came along—either alone or as a team. Another stage-struck, starry-eyed couple of dreamers setting out on the road to glory!

Chapter 9
Married Life In The Big Apple

Lovejean's show, as we laughingly called it, finished its tour and she returned to the City so we could get on with our plans. Our first one was to set the marriage date at June 11, 1949. We had friends, Paul and Hyla Jones, who lived in Greenwich Village and were members of a big, beautiful church called St. John's in the Village. It had a lovely courtyard surrounded by a full block of apartments, one of which was where the Jones lived, and was filled with large trees, bushes, and beautiful flowers, and there was a shrine just behind the church proper. A perfect place for a ceremony and that's where we decided to have it.

My old friend, Buddy Hackett, drove me to the wedding or I'm not sure I would have arrived...on time, at least. I had the "jitters" something fierce, not that I didn't want to get married, but just that I wasn't sure I wanted to do it now! I know that during the ceremony I cried, my nose ran, and I was a wreck, but it all came together somehow.

One of the guests at the wedding was the famous actor, John Carradine, and he, being a John Barrymore buff, had acquired the actual sword that Barrymore used in his great performance as "Hamlet." So, Carradine brought the sword along and we used it to cut the wedding cake! Actually, once I had recovered my cool, it turned out to be a very nice affair.

I, of course, was still doing *The 54th Street Revue,* but asked for a four-week hiatus so I could have a honeymoon. They allowed, and so our second plan was to decide where to go. Well, that wasn't a hard decision because we both wanted to go back to California and visit her Mom and her grandma, "Suckle" (from honeysuckle, they were from the South). We managed to stay at the beautiful Beverly Hills Hotel for the first week

Dick Jones, Gene Autry and Russ in *Sons of New Mexico*, 1949.

of our honeymoon, and when the money ran out we moved in with Mom and Suckle.

During that time I had contacted my old agent, Gus Dembling (bless his heart!), and he had gotten me a Gene Autry movie to do. I had done one other with Gene earlier on, so they took me back with no problems. The shooting schedule was only two weeks, so the timing was perfect. Worked out well cause the picture paid for the trip.

Incidentally, I had quite an adventure on this pic. I played the part of the cadet commander at the New Mexico Military Institute. The story concerned a young punk who needed a lot of discipline and was put into the school by Autry for that reason. The big deal at NMMI is their polo team, and I was captain of that team. All well and good, except that playing polo isn't like riding on a Western saddle, which I could do fine.

Polo calls for a little flat saddle and a double set of reins and, of course, a polo mallet in your other hand. In the story a kid is jealous of me because he's a great rider in his own right, but riding against the cadet commander and being the jealous punk he is, he wants to prove that he is the better man and so will stoop to anything to win.

In the game they shot, we had a lot of pushing, shoving, and bumping, to say nothing of him swinging at me with his polo mallet! After they took all the long shots of the match, we then came to the close-ups. By now it was getting late in the day and the sun was going down, so they were in a terrific hurry to get these final shots, the last of which was of me galloping into a camera close-up, pulling the horse up, looking around, taking a swing with my mallet and then heading off in a different direction. I had been riding a nice, comfortable, fat little mare and doing very well with her and all my equipment, but the ASPCA man on the set said we couldn't run the mare anymore because she was tired. (So was I!)

So, with the light getting dimmer (or "getting yellow" as they say in the pic business), they put me up on another horse and told me to back a-ways and come on a-galloping. I was willing, but the horse had different ideas! This was a skinny, hardheaded sucker that threw his head when you pulled up on the reins—all of which I didn't know because we had no time to have a practice run. The camera was almost buried in a little hole in the ground so they could get an upward shot of me as I stopped and looked around.

So I came a-gallopin' and, sure enough, as I pulled up he threw his head around and I felt myself coming loose! Knowing I was going, I kicked my feet out of the stirrups, turned loose of everything, and sailed right over the horse's head, the camera and crew who were on the ground, and lit about six feet further out. I was sort of prepared and was able to roll as I landed, so no damage done. But now I had to get right back up and do the shot again, which, fortunately, I was able to do right the second time, just as the sun went down. I was lucky on that one!

Meanwhile, back at the apartment...Here's a funny little story about Suckle. She didn't go out much and sat in a back room in her rocking chair with both ears open so as not to miss anything. Well, I had left to shoot on the pic that morning and had come home mid-afternoon, as we had finished early. Only Suckle was home, so, having some extra time, I took the opportunity to call some old friends, among them my old friend, Arlene Dahl, who had just gotten a big break in an upcoming movie. Now, in show business everyone always uses a lot of endearing terms— darling, honey, sweetheart, etc.—and so it was that in my conversation with Arlene I had called her "darling" without thinking much about it.

Well, after my phone calls, I went out to the store for a bit and when I got home I could tell everyone was home but found all the doors shut in every room. Not a sound was to be heard, and, thinking something terrible must have happened, I tiptoed around opening and closing doors very quietly and carefully until I came to the kitchen and there were Lovejean and Love (her mom). They both had long, sad faces and wouldn't talk to me! I asked what had happened and still couldn't get an answer until I finally grabbed Lovejean and took her into another room and demanded to know what was the matter!

Finally, midst tears and sighs, she told me that I had been making love over the phone to an old girlfriend! Of course, Suckle had heard, and misinterpreted my conversation with Arlene! It took a bit of doing, but I finally was able to convince everyone that it was only a show business "darling" and so I was once more in the good graces of the family!

Too soon the picture was over and it was time to go back to New York where a lot of changes were about to occur. First, we had to move because the apartment I had been subletting was no longer available. It wasn't quite as hard (or expensive) to move about New York in those days and we quickly found a new place down in the Village at No. One Christopher Street. We felt that address had quite a ring to it and were happy to move in, even if it was 15 floors up. Happily, they did have a working elevator, and it was the first place I'd lived in where I didn't have to walk up stairs! So that was our first change.

The second thing we wanted to do was to change Lovejean's name. It was a bit too syrupy for a marquee was the general feeling. Now it so happened that an old friend of Lovejean's was producing a fifteen-minute TV show, and when she called him and suggested that he program a contest to rename her, he agreed and worked it into his show for three weeks. Lots of suggestions came in, but the one she finally chose (with my approval, I might add) was Liza Palmer. And that is how she was known for the rest of her career.

The third change wasn't one we chose to do, but it happened anyway. After our return from the honeymoon, there had been some changes on good ol' *54th Street*. We had a new emcee, a comic whose big trademark gag was him saying at the end of a joke, "how do you think I feel!" Guess you had to be there, but it actually was kind of funny…sometimes. Not funny enough, though, because they did let me go, and, I'm kind of happy to report, the show didn't last very much longer. Made me feel like it was because they fired me, which wasn't true of course, but I liked to think so!

So now here we were, newly married and jobless! A spot a lot of you have been in, I bet. We decided to work as a singing team, if we could, and did a lot of auditions together, as well as some we each did alone. We did get some guest shots on local 15-minute shows of which there were many in those days. Shows like the Ilka Chase show, the Gloria Swanson show (where we had to use GREEN makeup because of the fluorescent light that was used to light the stage. I really hated to see myself in the mirror at that show!), the Roberta Quinlan show (she was a local piano player, and all I remember about that show was that she had very bad breath. Sorry, Roberta!), and a show called the *Versatile Varieties*, on which the well-known actress, Anne Francis, got her start—something to do with her great legs.

TV was interesting in those days because the producers and networks were really learning their craft, feeling their way, and trying to decide which way to do what. The possibilities were tremendous and lots of experimenting was going on - remember the green makeup! There was no Cable, no unions, no restrictions on anything. I remember doing shows on a 15-minute notice. I'd get a call and they would say, "hurry on over here we need a couple of songs," and I'd go and get maybe $25 for it. But it was fun, and if a friend happened to have a TV set and had happened to

Russ doing "the pitch"—and he didn't even smoke!

see you and told you about it, well, that was really something! It meant there really were some people out there watching!

After a period of time we did an audition for another network show, this time for ABC. We did this one as a team, as it was for a game show, and we would sing, do sketches, work with contestants, and just be all-round personalities. I wish all auditions had been as easy as this one.

We had hardly finished singing a song when the producer was discussing terms with us! And they weren't bad terms for those days: $150 a week for each of us! The show was called *Chance of a Lifetime* and starred the late John Reed King as the host, and then us, of course…ha! We wound up doing a year on the show and Liza started doing some live commercials on another show as well, so things were looking up!

During this period my old friend, Ted Fetter, from *The 54th Street Revue*, called and asked if I would like to do some live commercials on the *Hit Parade* TV show. He had moved onto BBD&O (Batten, Barton, Durstine, and Osborne), a big ad agency, and they were going to be the producers of that show as it moved over from radio to TV. The pay would be $50-a-shot, and so, of course, I said yes. They had gathered together a small stock company of young hopefuls who would be in these little production commercials each week.

Although I didn't smoke (and never did), we all had to carry around lighted cigarettes, but it turned out to be a lot of fun because each week we would be in a different situation—in college, on a cruise ship, at the malt shop, or whatever. I only know that I lived in mortal terror of the day I would take a drag (fake) and cough on camera! It never happened, I'm happy to say, but the pressure was sure there!

I did a number of weeks of these commercials until, one day, and I don't know what got into me, I decided that I didn't want to do "commercials" anymore, so I called Ted and told him I wanted to quit. He was wonderful about it and told me the door was always open if I wanted to come back, bless him for that!

About that time, Liza and I auditioned for a guest shot on a show called *The Show Goes On*, hosted by Robert Q. Lewis. The aim of the show was to find jobs in nightclubs or supper clubs for various acts. I remember we sang "I Don't Care If the Sun Don't Shine," for one thing, and I do remember we got the job! It was a week in the Sheraton Hotel in Providence, Rhode Island, and it turned out to be a delight. Along with our salary, we received a suite, on the hotel, to stay in while we did the job!

Our first supper club job and they treated us like royalty! A wonderful way to be introduced into another world—nightclubs. But I'll get into that action a bit later in the book. Right now we are still doing TV.

One funny incident occurred during the *Chance of a Lifetime* show. The late Dennis James (a great guy) was the announcer and did live commercials, too. They had a well-known commercial for Old Gold cigarettes (one of our sponsors) with a pair of dancing cigarette packs. Two girl dancers would don the packs and all you could see of them were their legs, and, all the while, Dennis would be reading the copy plugging the product.

One night during this commercial his mind must have been somewhere else because at the end of the copy he said, "So be sure and smoke LUCKY STRIKES!" Fortunately, at that point, he was to go off stage, which he quickly did. At the next commercial break he rather sheepishly stuck his head through the curtain and said to the audience, "I'll bet you didn't expect to see me back!" I'm happy to report they didn't fire him for the goof. Such were the perils of LIVE TV.

We'd been on *Chance of a Lifetime* for a while, and I suddenly recovered my senses. I called Ted Fetter and asked him if I could come back and do the same Lucky Strike commercials again, and, thankfully, he said I could. Glad I did, too, because *Lifetime* was about to end and these commercials would lead to much better things for me.

In the meantime, Liza auditioned for the new *Kay Kyser Kollege of Musical Knowledge* show that was about to go on the air. And she was hired! Also, she was doing live commercials on another show, the *Major Bowes Amateur Hour*, for Swanson Frozen Foods. The only problem with that was that we didn't have a big enough freezer in order to take advantage of their generous offer for us to go to the warehouse and take what we'd like for our home use. Darn!

So things were going along swimmingly and we were very happy. But that was about to change, too. I have always held the belief that things go in cycles, so if you're really down, just wait a bit and it will all change for the better. And, conversely, if things are going really well, don't get too happy because it just might swing downwards again. And my theory was just about to prove right.

On the Kyser show all had gone well for Liza for several weeks when an agent from one of the big talent and production agencies was assigned to this show and suddenly got the "hots" for Liza. He asked her out, although he knew that we had recently been married and she was not interested. So when she refused his advances he threatened to "get her off the show," and he managed to do it! In spite of all we could do, she was gone.

Accepting it all with a heavy heart, she continued to go to auditions, trying to find other shows to do. On one such audition she was asked to go to a suite in one of New York's finest hotels as the man she was auditioning for was in a big hurry. (An old dodge if I've ever heard one!) But, she went anyway, and was met by the gentleman (?) in his robe, beneath which he wore absolutely nothing. He happened to be one of the most successful songwriters and arrangers then working, and this made it even harder to believe he'd stoop to this. So he chased her around the suite, though I'm happy to report he didn't catch her, and she left hurt and disappointed. She still had the Swanson commercials, but, alas, they were to end shortly and we were left with just my Lucky Strike commercials.

So back we went to my friend, Ted, and to BBD&O, where a whole new life was about to begin!

Chapter 10
The Hit Parade Days

I didn't really know what would happen when I went back to the Lucky Strike commercials; I just knew I had a job. But it turned out to be a whole lot more than that.

The American Tobacco Company, the makers of Luckies, ran the *Hit Parade* show with an iron fist. After all, it had been on radio for more than 20 years and had been extremely successful. Now that it was on TV, too, they of course wanted it to be just as successful in the new medium. So everything concerned with the show had to be cleared with their office "downtown." That very word could cause fear and trembling in the hearts of any of the production people, to say nothing of the cast!

As I rejoined the commercial cast, the main show consisted of a wonderful orchestra led by Raymond Scott (the brother of Mark Warnow, who, after leading the band for many years on radio, had died) and three star singers. They were Dorothy Collins, the newest of the three and, also coincidentally, Raymond Scott's wife; Snooky Lanson, a "good ol' southern boy"; and Eileen Wilson, who had been on the radio show along with Snooky. So it was a "three-star" show. The producer was with BBD&O, the big ad agency, and was a fine gentleman by the name of Dan Lounsberry. Our director at that time was Clark Jones, an old standby at NBC, and, incidentally, an excellent director.

We did the show from Rockefeller Center but not in the studios. There used to be a big theater as a part of the complex at the corner of 6th Avenue (as it was then, now Avenue of the Americas) and I believe 48th Street. It was at that theater the show was produced. We had a live audience; just a regular theatrical show.

It was a bit crowded backstage, and there were little dressing areas just off to each side of the stage where everyone had to make the fast changes the show sometimes required, so it wasn't unusual for flashes of flesh to be seen, although we were all so busy and hurried that no one seemed to notice. Getting ready for the next number was the most important thing! However, I must admit that even being in a hurry I did notice a bit from time to time—shame on me!

I had been doing the commercials regularly and all was going well when one week we did a circus scene. I played a Keystone Kop, using all the funny moves they used to do, and my performance caught the eye of someone "downtown." They had decided to have a general understudy for the show because one week Snooky, who lived out in Westchester County, almost didn't get to the show because of a huge snowstorm and they wanted to cover the possibility that it might happen again. So, the search for an understudy was on.

Again, my friend, Ted Fetter, came to my rescue. He called and asked if I would like to audition for the spot. Well, I happened to know that they were also looking for an announcer-type to do some filmed commercials, so I asked Ted if I could audition for both things. He demurred, saying that they were looking for real announcers, but, having done some of that sort of work in the past, I insisted, so he said he'd see what he could do.

What he managed to do was to have me sing two songs on a kinescope (which was merely 16mm film) and after the other hopefuls had done their stuff, he let me read some copy for the commercials.

I thanked him profusely and went home to await the results. They were not long in coming. American Tobacco signed me to a contract to be the general understudy for the show, which meant that I would have to cover ALL the songs each week and be ready to jump in if the need arose. They would pay me $400 a week and there was a promise that I would do some film commercials, for an additional fee, from time to time!

So, the next year, I was a busy boy! I did get to do some filmed commercials (oh, those residual checks raining gently down in the mail!), but the main thing I had to do was to be at every rehearsal and LEARN a lot of things…I mean a LOT of things! You see, they never asked if you could do a particular thing, they just said this week you WOULD do it, whatever it was, dancing of all sorts (you should have seen me in ballet tights), or singing Rock (not my preference), we had to do it all, whatever came along. What a great training ground!

Snooky, Dorothy and Russ with June Valli who was with us for one year.

I want to add a side note here. People have often asked me if working on the show was as much fun as it looked and if everyone liked each other as much as they seemed to on camera. The answer is a qualified "yes." I say "qualified" because when you have a group of performers jockeying for position, you're bound to have some upsets—disagreements, hurt feelings, etc.

On the show was a group of singers and another group of dancers. One of the singers was a fella named Joe Pryor, a good singer and a fair actor, who was very popular with the cast. So when the understudy role was up for grabs, Joe tried out for it and everyone was rooting for him to get it. However, I got it and became a "bad guy" for taking the part away from their friend, Joe. There was no overt anger directed toward me, but the feeling was there, no doubt about it. It took quite a while for the feeling to go away and for them to accept me, but I'm happy to say that they finally did and I never had any problems with anyone, well, except maybe Snooky, but I'll get to that in a bit.

The producers made another change about that time. They decided to replace Eileen Wilson with June Valli, a popular record star of the time. Whoever knows the reasons for changes like this, but they do occur. So, the year I was the understudy, June was also a newcomer who had to "break in" with the group, and, as a result, she and I became good buddies and helped each other out with our mutual feelings of not quite belonging. We remained good friends until her untimely death a few years later.

So now, in effect, there was a new show. I did go to every rehearsal and was chomping at the bit to be allowed to do a number on the air, but no luck! Finally, on the last show of the year, word came down from on high (downtown) that I should be given a number as a "thank you" for all the hard work I had put in. What excitement and what a thrill! I was actually going to be on the air! Then I found out what song I was going to sing, and HOW they were going to stage it.

The song was fine, "My Truly, Truly Fair," a nice, bright tune, made popular by the big record star, Guy Mitchell. So far, so good, but then came the crusher. The song was to be done by me and a group of tramps in a boxcar, and the makeup consisted of grubby, dirty, full whiskers while the costumes were ragged, dirty suits, and I had a big hat to cover the part of my face the whiskers missed! I really felt they did it on Joe's behalf—getting even for my getting "his" spot or something like that. Or maybe they were just checking to see that I would be able to deliver a real performance under pressure. Maybe all that wasn't true, but it sure felt like it.

However, my angel was still sitting on my shoulder. As I mentioned, that was the last show of that particular season, and during the summer hiatus of 13 weeks a lot of fan mail came in asking WHO that was singing "Truly Fair?" There was enough mail to intrigue the folks "downtown," and they sent word that I was to be used whenever possible in the new season. So, in spite of everything, I was going to be on the air occasionally. Talk about working one's way up from the bottom!

I might as well say right here that, although I wasn't aware of it, my biggest problem about getting on the air was good ol' Snooky. Every time something good happened for me and I advanced just a little bit on the show, he would go downtown to some of his southern friends and put in a complaint. It worked to some extent because my progress, though steady, was slow. Thinking it over, I can't say that I blame him. After all, he had had the show to himself as the only male singer and didn't welcome the thought of having a rival to worry about. And, frankly, we did get along well together.

For instance, if a new song like "Davy Crockett," with its endless verses and tons of words, got on the show, we would help each other out, if we could, by holding a cue card for the other guy until we got the words down. Cue cards, as such, were not allowed on the show because of the staging of the numbers. There just wasn't room or time enough for such niceties. The feeling was that it wasn't too much to ask the performers to learn the lyrics, and I agree, in principal. But there were times when it just became a bit much to remember the lyrics, plus the staging, hitting the right spots, etc. So, Snooky and I would help each other out if we could.

Speaking of cues, we all did one other thing. If we needed help with words on a new song, we would often jot down bits of the lyric wherever we could—in the palm of a hand, inside a hat, on any prop we were using - anywhere! I remember one week that Snooky had a song and was having trouble with the lyrics.

He was sitting at an outdoor café in Paris as the setting, and he had written a few cues for himself on the tablecloth out of sight of the camera. Everything went well through dress rehearsals, and then, as we were back in our dressing rooms repairing makeup and costumes for the real show, an eager-beaver stagehand went through the sets to make sure all was in order and ready to go. He got to the outdoor café set and noticed what to him was a smudge on the tablecloth. So he carefully turned the table cloth over where it was nice and clean!

Now we fast forward to the actual show and Snooky hurrying to his set where he had been all prepared, only to discover his lyrics were gone and he had no time to do anything about it. I don't know what lyrics he sang, and I'm sure he didn't either, but that was the chance one took when doing live TV. You got ONE shot and if you blew it, there went your week!

I had a problem when a new Elvis Presley song came on the show. I was to sing "Blue Suede Shoes" and, for the life of me, couldn't get the lyrics. They made no sense to me whatsoever, but I did my best. Comes show time, and I completely blew the words, but I just keep smiling and singing SOMETHING, and nobody knew the difference! There was some puzzlement among the production people, but I just kept smiling and insisting that what I sang were the right words. I really had no idea what I sang, but I got away with it.

There are endless stories about things that happened on the show. Remember we had to deal with the time element, too. The show was only a half-hour, and every second had something squeezed into it.

The production values of the show were really way ahead of their time. Our choreographer, who was then Tony Charmoli, did the actual staging and had his hands full, but he did an excellent job.

We had now moved into our permanent studio, 8H, on the eighth floor of the NBC building. We felt impressed because this was the same studio from which Arturo Toscanini had done his famous NBC Symphony radio broadcasts. They had even kept his dressing room just like it was when he had been there, almost like a shrine. Of course it was sealed off and only shown to visiting dignitaries, so I never did get to see that.

But there was no room for an audience in the studio, just a few seats in a balcony where special invited guests might come and watch. Before we had moved from the theater, they had recorded the audience applauding and laughing, etc. a number of times so that, in the future, we could use those sound tracks in our show. So we were really being applauded by our own audience.

The band was set up near the center of the studio and sets for the various songs were placed strategically throughout the studio, with a mike for the announcer (Andre Baruch, who was excellent and had been with the show for more than 20 years, including the radio days), and other mikes for the background singers who filled in as the principals did their numbers.

It was quite a sight in the middle of the studio because the singers would be changing for the next number even as they sang for the present one. And, all the while, the hairdresser would be working on hair changes and makeup people would be fixing lipstick, powdering, etc. and, yet, somehow, with all this confusion, the next number would go on as scheduled and with perfect aplomb!

Each Monday a luncheon would be scheduled "downtown" with all the production people as well as the liaison tobacco people who were concerned with the show. They had received a copy of the survey of songs telling them what was number one and which ones followed in what order. It was at this meeting that the songs were assigned to the stars for the week, and the production people would explain how they wanted the numbers staged.

Sometimes that would be a bit difficult because a certain number, oh, "Harbor Lights" for instance, would stay on the survey for a long time, maybe 15 weeks, and it had to be staged in a different way each week. They had three stars, and now me once in a while, so they were able to make a difference that way, but they had to remember the different styles of the singers and try to assign songs that would be best suited to that particular singer.

Also, once in a while it happened that the production people would have a setting all worked out and, for some reason, the tobacco liaison person didn't like it. Of course, that was the end of that! There would be much scurrying around, and an alternative setting would quickly be suggested which, hopefully, would be approved.

On Monday afternoon we singers would call in to find out what we were going to sing that week so we could learn the song if it was a new one, or just refresh it in our minds if we'd done it before. On Tuesday, the dancers (and the principal, if it was going to be a big production number) would go into rehearsal and on Wednesday the principals would go in for their staging rehearsal. Thursday would be further rehearsal and a trip to the costumer, if that was necessary.

And on Friday morning we would go into a different studio and sing the numbers with the band, with particular emphasis on new numbers or duets or group numbers. Then, Friday afternoon, we went into still another studio where all the sets had been chalked out on the floor and the cameramen, director, and choreographer would all follow us as we walked through the actual camera moves (but without the camera) while we sang the numbers to a rehearsal piano. On Saturday morning we would report to studio 8H and work all day with the actual camera staging. After a dinner break, about eight o'clock, would come the dress rehearsal to finalize everything for the actual show at 10:30 Saturday night. Quite a week! It was a wonderful mixture of work—fun, games, and personalities!

Chapter 11
Fun, Games and Personalities

At the end of my year as understudy, I felt that I had served my apprenticeship and wanted to be promoted to the same level as the others. Two big things rankled. One, I wasn't included in the introductions through the Lucky Strike bull's-eye and I didn't get to sing the #1 song in my turn. So, I requested a meeting with the production people, again through my friend Ted.

Instead of meeting with Ted as I had hoped, another negotiator from BBD&O called and invited me to lunch at Sardi's, one of my favorite eateries because of its showbiz ambiance. So, off I went without realizing that I was about to indulge in one of the famous "martini" lunches the ad world is so famous for. The gentleman, whose name escapes me at the moment, was very used to this sort of thing, and later on as I heard, had to be treated for alcoholism. So, I was at a distinct disadvantage. All I wanted was to be heard!

So lunch (or rather the martinis) proceeded and the discussion began. I soon realized that he was picking my brain about the show and what problems there might be. I tried to get my points across but mostly I wound up answering questions. I dimly remember eating something and soon found myself out on 44th Street blinking in the sunlight and wondering what had happened.

I do remember my saying that if I didn't receive equal treatment I would probably leave the show! His incredulous question in answer to that was, "YOU WOULD LEAVE THE HIT PARADE??" "Well, no," I mumbled, "I don't want to leave the show, but I do feel strongly that I should be considered on an equal basis with the others." His answer was an indifferent chuckle but I had at least made a stand and now was wondering if I would regret it.

Most fortunately, I did not regret it. We were near the summer hiatus and, after a meeting downtown, word came down that the next season would be different. They would make it a four-star show and I would be considered as one of the stars! And, incidentally, they made another change; June Valli was let go and they hired Gisele MacKenzie in her place. So, now the four stars that most everyone considered as "The TV Hit Parade" were in place: Dorothy, Snooky, Gisele, and Russ. Happy Days!

I promised to discuss some of the personalities of the cast, so I shall

Dorothy Collins and Russ in a version of "Allegheny Moon" on *Your Hit Parade.*

start with Dorothy Collins. I loved her! She was one of the most considerate, caring, loving people I have ever met, and I don't think anyone had a bad word to say about her. For instance, if anyone had a birthday, and I mean anyone, either in the cast or the production staff, she was first in line with a cake and a present. She was always sending cards for special occasions and was a genuinely nice person. Of course, she was married to Raymond Scott, the bandleader, and he fought her battles for her. As he was a part of every production meeting that was some formidable backing, so she could afford to be nice. I don't mean that in a bad way, those were just the facts. Much, much later in my life after a lot of things happened, and which I will cover later in the book, there was a good possibility that we might have married. So you can see that I really thought she was something special!

Now comes Snooky. He was the kind of guy you just couldn't dislike. He was a good ol' southern boy and just oozed charm and politeness. In spite of the fact that he didn't want me on the show, we got along quite well. He did what he could to protect his spot which is perfectly understandable, but on the few occasions that we socialized we had a good time together. I remember standing at a bar with him at one of the country clubs in New York and his saying to me, "You son of a bitch; I like you in spite of everything!" And I answered in kind! His clout came from having been with the TV show from the beginning, even before that on radio, and his friendship with the southern tobacco people who, after all, had the final say on what happened on the show. So, if he had a problem, he could always run "downtown" and discuss it. Pretty good clout, I'd say!

As far as Gisele is concerned, we remained friends until she passed away. She was a wonderful singer and LOVED performing. However, when it came to doing a duet with her, as I did several times, just watch out because the camera became her sole aim. I remember once during a rehearsal saying to her, as she was supposedly singing to me but had her face directly in the camera instead of looking at me, "Hey, I'm over here!" I got instant response from the director's booth to cut it out.

They loved her no matter what. She was a very good performer, I must say, and her clout came from having a personal manager who also went to every production meeting and stoutly defended her position, whatever the case. I'm still very, very fond of the lady and wished her nothing but good!

So now we come to Russ—that's me. I came in the back door, for sure, and really had to work hard for everything I got. I always say that the public was my only clout. I did get a lot of fan mail and recognition from the fans, and I think that was noticed by those "downtown," plus I met some tobacco wives and daughters on occasion and felt a definite warmth, so maybe they helped, too. I know I had one good thing going for me. They did a lot of costume numbers on the show, tights and all that, and with my theatrical background I knew how to wear them in style. Also, I was told by a number of fans that I had great legs...ha! I'm not boasting, but just looking for reasons as to why good things continued to happen for me.

I was once told by one of the production people that when they came up with an idea that they didn't particularly like or was difficult to stage they would give it to me, if possible, because they knew I could handle most anything or, at least, could give it a good try.

I think it might be appropriate along about here to mention some of the funny things that we were called on to do, all the while singing. I remember an incident when Snooky and Gisele were playing a couple of hillbillies in a rundown cabin. It was his birthday and she had baked him a cake. Well, they had put frosting on a balloon to represent the cake and, of course, it had to

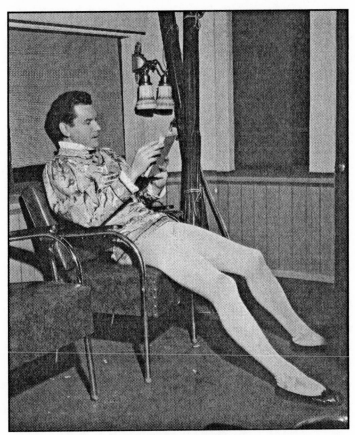

Relaxing at rehearsal.

happen on the air, somehow the balloon got punctured! Just as he was about to cut it, or pretend to, the air oozed out of the cake and there he was with a flat pancake. Maybe you had to be there, but it was hilarious, and they could hardly contain themselves until the number was over!

One week I sang while on water skis. Of course we were in the studio but there I was in my trunks, actually standing in the skis, holding onto to a rope that a stagehand was pulling on while another was spraying me with very cold water. We were doing all this in front of a movie screen which was the background, and I also had to watch a third stagehand who was directing me which way to lean to correspond with the film on the screen! And they wondered why we might forget an occasional lyric!

Another time I was playing a cowboy and singing "Your Cold, Cold Heart." It was a very dramatic setting with a set built like a two-story western house. My girl was up in the window with another cowboy and they were oblivious of me standing down below on the ground 'cause they were kissing and doing all that good stuff. I, of course, was very jealous and, while singing, mounted some stairs on the outside of the house and pulled my gun to get my vengeance on the other guy for taking my gal.

Just as I finished the song, I was supposed to shoot him, but he was too fast and he shot me, instead. So I got to do a dramatic death scene and fall from the top of the stairs! The only thing was that it was at least a six-foot drop to the very hard floor of the stage.

When I used to do Western pics I had a stunt double to do this sort of thing for me, but here I had to do it myself. Well, I managed, but it was a bit scary. Again, when you had to think about falling correctly, etc., it made it a little tough to concentrate on lyrics!

But there were special stagings, too. For instance, one week we did the show from the beautiful ocean liner, the S.S. *UNITED STATES*, which was in port at that time. How wonderful it was to work from those gorgeous decks! I vividly remember singing the moody, romancing song "I'll Walk Alone" while strolling along the promenade deck and looking out over the harbor. A true thrill!

The worst thing that happened accidentally was on our famous Christmas show which was the highlight of the year and was always staged down under the huge Christmas tree in Rockefeller Center.

The big finale was the singing of "O, Holy Night" and this year Snooky was to do it. All well and good, except that while they staged the action down there, the band, being too big to move down eight floors for just one number, was still up in the regular studio on the eighth floor with the music being piped down to speakers at the ice rink level.

The scene had unfolded with all four of us singing "Mr. Sandman" in a big sleigh right on the rink. So, as the number finished, and while they cut to a commercial, Snooky had to get out of the sleigh, run across the ice, climb a couple of small sets of stairs, run through a small pathway and position himself under the tree for the song. And to add to the confusion, it was snowing!

Well, by the time Snooky could get himself positioned to start singing, the band had already started with the introduction for "O, Holy Night." Now this particular intro is a difficult one, at best, 'cause you have to count the bars of music to know just where you are, and it was almost impossible for Snooky to hear with all the confusion and the running and everyone else taking their places on each side of his spot, so he had no idea where they were in the intro. Finally, in desperation, he just took a deep breath and

Being fitted for "Lady of Spain" on *Your Hit Parade.*

started to sing, and, unfortunately, it was at the wrong spot.

Our vocal coach, Ray Charles (no, not *that* Ray Charles), had seen what was coming and had lain down in the slush-covered pathway, in his beautiful cashmere overcoat, to be out of camera range, and was desperately trying to give Snooky the correct place in the music. Finally, after what seemed like an eternity, it all came together and he and the rest of us were able to finish the song and the show.

Immediately thereafter, Snooky disappeared and wouldn't talk with anyone, for which no one could blame him—the highlight of the year, and this had to happen! It was just unfortunate logistics! But the capper to the story is this. Next day in the paper one of the critics picked up on it in his column (not knowing what had actually happened) and said that "the usually reliable RUSSELL ARMS forgot the words to the Christmas song on the *Hit Parade* last night." So, even though I had nothing to do with it, I got the blame! Sometimes ya' just can't win!

Chapter 12

Career Growth

The Christmas season was always a happy one, and especially this one because we were all together, finally. New York is always at her best at the Christmas season because the snow looks so lovely, and stores are all beautifully lit and decorated for this special time of year. And, of course, there are all the parties and gatherings that take place. We, as a group, were invited "downtown" to the head offices of the American Tobacco Company, to meet with, and sing for, the officers and employees of the company. This was very exciting for me because I had never been there or met those folks before.

Upon our arrival, we were greeted cordially by several of the officers of the company who offered us food and drink. Before we sang, one of the vice-presidents took us on a tour of the main offices with pictures of all the past presidents and other brass hung on every wall. He was explaining how it all worked and, during this, he suddenly offered me a cigarette!

Well, Snooky was the only one of the four of us who smoked, and I wondered just how I was going to tell the VP this, so I falteringly said, "I'm sorry, sir, but I…don't…smoke." As he took back the cigarette pack, I had visions of my career going down the drain, but he paused a second, and, looking rather stern, finally said with a smile, "Well, that's okay, but if you ever do smoke, you'd better smoke THESE!" And he wasn't kidding! One thing they never fooled around about was "the product."

Fortunately, just about then the tour finished and Raymond Scott called us to do the singing bit we had prepared. Actually, it turned out to be a very nice evening with good food and lots of compliments from the secretaries and workers present, but it was a bit of a relief when it was over. Talk about trying to be on one's best behavior!

That was the only time I visited the home office until the day they called us all in to fire us, a couple of years later. But that's another story, which we'll get to in due time.

The weeks went by very fast because they were so full. You were never asked if you could do a certain thing, they just said, "This week you will be…whatever…" For instance, one week they had me in ballet tights partnering one of our dancers in some ballet moves, and, of course, singing all the while. I think the song was "Change Partners," which was very apropos, come to think of it! Anyway, there I was trying my best to look like a ballet dancer, and, I must say, my acting background really helped me in situations like that. I just PLAYED a ballet dancer and somehow it seemed to work out!

Being on the shy side (no kidding), I found myself in a situation one week that I didn't know how to handle. The scene was on a beach, just me and my girl. I was working with a model named Nadine who I'd worked with a number of times before and who was a great gal. We were seated among some coconut palms in the sand, and I was to lean over her and sing and look very romantic.

It would have been all right except that, even though my position was very awkward for me, it seemed to be the only one that satisfied the camera and lighting guys, so that's how it had to be. However, in order to lean over her properly I had to prop myself on one arm and my hand had to be between her legs and right up against her. (I blush to think of it even today.) I apologized and explained that if my hand wasn't right there, I'd fall over on her, as I leaned in to sing. She was a trooper and understood the problem and told me to go ahead and lean and sing. So, I did, and I'm sure it looked very romantic, but I'm just glad the audience couldn't tell what was going on in my mind! I sent her flowers after the show to thank her—for understanding, I mean!

Incidentally, the *HP* production people managed to use Liza several times as someone I sang to, instead of using a model. One week she and I did "True Love" in which she got to sing the Grace Kelly part and that was very special because, although she was enjoying being "Mrs. Russell Arms" as I got to be better known, she really missed her own career.

After some time had passed, we talked it over and decided that we should move because we wanted to be a little more out in the country (faux California) instead of hearing subway cars 15 floors up, so we went out to Flushing on Long Island.

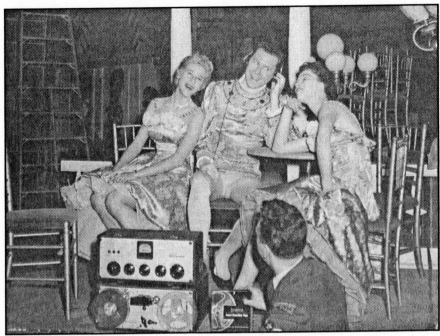

Russ and 2 friends performing "How Much Is That Doggie in the Window?"

It was at the end of a subway line and was as far as we could go without having to live by a train schedule. We had what was called a "garden apartment" because there was a bit of lawn at the entrance to the place, but it did give us the feeling of being out of the city, yet close in. It took a little more time to get to work but we felt it was worth it.

I mentioned before about my favorite restaurant, Sardi's. We used to go in quite often because of the theatrical ambiance and so we got to know the owner, Vincent, quite well. I had decided to give a "spread" for the *Hit Parade* people and so arranged with Vincent to have it in their upstairs party room. They were wonderful about it and did all the necessary planning.

All I had to do was provide the numbers and tell them how much I wanted to spend per person on food and drink. It took a little figuring but I managed to work it out, and so it was that on a particular Sunday afternoon everybody showed up and we had a wonderful time, even had some impromptu singing and dancing and lots of good cheer. I did this because I wanted to remind everyone that I was now a real member of the cast, and I think it was worth it, because from then on there was a slightly different attitude toward me from most everyone.

Maybe I was just being sensitive, but, to me, there was still a slight hangover of the attitudes from the first days of my being with the show. Now it seemed to loosen up and everyone seemed to accept me whole-heartedly, which was what I was after. I fondly recall that afternoon and evening at Sardi's, and, as it turned out, it didn't cost all that much either!

We always had 13 weeks off during the summer as a hiatus period, and that, of course, meant we would all scramble to find work for that time. It wasn't too difficult because by now we were all quite well known both in the business and by the public, so we would book other TV shows, nightclubs, fairs, dinner theaters, etc....anything to keep busy.

My first summer, I started out by doing the Cole Porter musical, *Anything Goes* for two weeks just outside of Chicago. My girlfriend in that was played by a very young and eager Carol Lawrence, long before she became a Broadway star in *West Side Story*.

My next stop was Reno, Nevada, for a nightclub appearance at the Golden Hotel for a week. That was special because I got to work with the fantastic Shecky Greene, a comedian who was most unusual, to say the least. Once he got going, and if the audience was "with" him, you couldn't get him off! He was really hysterical!

Once we went out gambling after our show and he gave me $300 of his to keep with the instructions that I was not to give it back to him under any circumstances. All went well for a while as he was winning, but when he started to lose he asked me for his money. I told him that, as per his instructions, he couldn't have it and I thought that would be the end of it. No way! He became a madman and threw a fit, threatened me with bodily harm, etc. I finally tossed him the money and left. When I saw him again the next night at the show, it was as though it had never happened. However, I never held cash for him again. He was hysterical, I guess. in more ways than one! But I really enjoyed working with him.

Now back to other summer jobs. I was booked into a lovely little nightclub in Columbia, South Carolina, for two weeks and, never having been in the South before, wanted to try the local foods. However, after my first attempt at grits, red-eye gravy, etc., I decided to stick with more familiar fare! But the club was delightful, and the people couldn't have been nicer, so it more than made up for my dietary problems.

One number I sang in my show was "Birth of the Blues" and I made a little production out of it. I'd have all the blue lights turned on, and, as I wore a midnight blue tux, the effect was, you might say, "bluesy." I did the verse first, ad lib, and had a trumpet play blue-fills after each line as I took a lot of time to get out a Lucky Strike cigarette (though, as you may remember, I didn't smoke, so this was just for effect). I'd pat myself down looking for a match, which I never found, would then look up to find one of the pretty local gals (who I had hired from the club) approach with a lit match for me. After lighting up and kissing the gal on the cheek, I would finally start the song.

One night, just as I got ready to start the real singing, from out of the darkened blue room came a female voice crying, "Oh, his eyes are so blue!" It broke everyone up, including me, but I managed to get through the rest of the song with further incident. The week went by very quickly and enjoyably.

From there, Liza and I took a three-day break and went to a very posh place, Sea Island, Georgia. It was quite fancy and plush and many of the brass from Washington, including presidents, took their holidays there. It was really most impressive, especially because this was the first time I had never stayed at a place where you hung your breakfast menu on your door-knob and it was delivered at a specified time as your wake-up call. Nice!

But I've always had trouble with being posh, just never got the hang of it. So, while there, instead of playing tennis or having tea and lying around the pool or some such, Liza and I went over to the little dock they had, rented a rowboat and spent our time fishing. Caught some, too! We took them into the cook who prepared them beautifully for our dinner. Just common folk, that's us!

After Sea Island, I went back to work. I was to sing three nights for the Wilson Cruise Line out of Washington, D.C., on a ship that cruised up and down the Potomac River. The object of the cruise was to get to a little island a ways downstream where they had gambling, legal or not, I never knew. I simply sang one show going and one coming back and enjoyed myself immensely. And they paid me handsomely, too!

It was getting close to the opening of the new *HP* season, so we headed back to New York where I did three "club dates." These are one-shot deals where you walk in with your charts in your hand, introduce yourself to the pianist and/or band, sing for about an hour, and hope for the best from the music. Usually it works out pretty well because these musicians do a lot of shows and so know all the current music as well as the old standards. If a problem comes up, you simply "wing it." There's not much pressure, so I always just relaxed, sang my best, and had fun.

Sometimes it was almost enough if you just showed up. They were so happy to have a real live "name" performer there in person, that the show itself didn't matter that much. They were happy to have you there signing autographs, having a drink with them, and taking personal snapshots with your arm in theirs. It all made for a good time!

Some amazing things happened while doing personal appearances, both at home in New York City or on the road, as we shall see!

Chapter 13

Onwards and Upwards

The *Hit Parade* show got more important as time went by. Our production people were extremely inventive, and week after week produced unusual settings for the songs, as well as unusual stagings in those settings. Of course that wasn't true of every song, but many of them were outstanding.

When we had the time, we often went to other cities to make appearances on local TV shows, and, when I did, it made me very proud to have the staff of that station gather around and ask questions about how our productions were staged and how the camera shots were set up, as well as a lot of technical questions that I had no answer for! That happened a number of times, and I found they were asking about things that I was taking for granted as a normal way of doing things. More credit to our production staff for being ahead of the times.

Such was early TV, though. Everyone was feeling their way and trying to develop the medium into something special. I don't mean to brag, but our people were unique in the way they used the cameras, in their staging of numbers, and in the ideas they came up with for the backgrounds of the songs. So much so that people in the TV industry took notice and, eventually, we won every award they were giving in those days.

The third year I was on the show we got a new director and choreographer. Bill Colleran now directed and Ernie Flatt did the staging and choreography, and both did great jobs. The show had a professional look and that attitude carried over into rehearsals. Although it was great fun to do, there was no fooling around because of time limitations. Our singers and dancers were excellent and did some outstanding work. Modestly, I like to think the stars did the same.

Everyone contributed and made the show one to be proud of and one that got a lot of recognition from both the general public and in the TV field—hence, all the awards! The night we won the Emmy was extra special! We stood in line at the end of the show to sing "So Long for a While" and passed the trophy from hand to hand. As we did so, I have to say, it was hard to let go!

You must remember that this was still fairly early in TV history and we were shooting in black and white or as we laughingly called it "living black and white," a spoof of the NBC logo of "in living color."

NBC, as well as the rest of the industry, was working very hard to make color viable, and we actually did two or three shows in early color, but that was really still in the future. We didn't even have coast-to-coast cable yet, although the cable did go through while we were still on the air, and it was a very exciting night when we actually covered the whole country at once! As I recall, that was in 1955.

Our show was broadcast live from Rockefeller Center at 10:30 p.m. on Saturday nights. It went as far as Chicago, where they made a Kine-scope of the show. That film was then shipped to the West and aired the following week, so out there it was actually a week behind the original broadcast, not that it mattered. The Kines were then shipped back to New York where NBC destroyed them, for lack of storage space.

Fortunately for me, one of the shipping clerks was an aspiring songwriter and asked me to make some demos of his songs, for which he would clip out some of my songs from the Kines that were to be destroyed and give them to me. I was delighted to do it, of course, and he did come up with three or four reels of me in action which I had transferred to videotape and have to this day. When I look back on them now, I'm still proud of a lot of the work, but I have a hard time recognizing me up there! It's hard to think of yourself as "history" when you're still alive and kicking!

About this time I got a manager, in addition to my agent. His name was Mike Stewart and he was very well known in the music business. He managed The Four Lads, a very popular singing group of that time, as well as Johnny Ray of "Cry" fame, and two very sweet Italian gals, the DeJohn Sisters, who also had a few hits along the way. And now he had me! Well, it did make a big difference for me 'cause he immediately got me a record contract with Epic Records, a subsidiary of Columbia.

I was thrilled and delighted and looking forward to my first record-ing session. It wasn't long in coming, and I was particularly happy because

I was able to get some of the *Hit Parade* singers for my backup on the date. With all those familiar faces, I felt very comfortable in the studio. We did one song, "The Touch," which I was sure would be a hit. (I still like it!) But it was "covered" by seven other artists, meaning they recorded it, too, and while it got a lot of play, its effect was dissipated because so many artists were singing it. One needs the concentration on one artist for a record to take off, so, unfortunately, not much happened with it for me.

I did two more sessions with Epic, and this introduced me to the crazy world of the recording industry, with all that entails: traveling to promote your record, seeing the disc jockeys who were all-powerful in getting your record on the air, trying to get your record on jukeboxes, guesting on local TV shows for the purpose of singing your new record, and even...payola! That was the reason so many deejays got very wealthy in a hurry.

The government finally stepped in and stopped the practice, but it was rampant at the time. I didn't get involved personally with anything other than singing the records and going out to promote them, but Mike knew his way around the business and did what he had to, I suppose.

Before one had a hit record it was sometimes difficult to get in to see a deejay. They were too busy or had someone else scheduled or had a million other reasons for not seeing you. I spent a lot of time waiting in outer offices, but I had good company, people like Johnny Mathis and Pat Boone were also cooling their heels.

However, if you had a hot record you were in the studio and talking on the air almost before you got your coat off! What a difference a hit record made! I know because I had switched labels and now recorded for Era Records in California, and almost immediately got my first hit! (And, I have to ruefully add, my ONLY hit!)

It was a little Spanish waltz called "Cinco Robles," and it made a huge difference in my professional life. It did sell a million copies but I never got a "gold record." It hung on the wall of the Era record company, and that's where it stayed! Many years later, my dear wife Mary Lynne MADE me a gold record and that one hangs on my wall to this day. So there!

However, one very important side effect it had was to jump my salary in nightclubs and personal appearances. I had been getting $750 a week until "Cinco," but after that it jumped to $1,750 with no trouble at all!

I must mention one of my favorite cities right here: Boston. For some reason, I did very well in that town. One of my first nightclub dates was there, and I subsequently went back there two more times. My record was very big there, and I was able to do a lot of guest shots on radio and TV shows. One of the Boston newspapers published a chart they kept of hit records. There were six columns representing six different deejays, and one week "Cinco Robles" was number one in all six columns! I really felt on top of the world that week!

Later on, I was to emcee three Miss World USA beauty pageants, and two of them were in Boston. I have a couple of funny stories about them which I'll tell you about a bit later.

I mentioned my salary in clubs. That, combined with my *Hit Parade* salary, put me into a pretty good bracket, for those days at least. However, I must explain something, and this applies to most of the big salaries in the business. I had an agent that cost me 10%, a manager that cost 20%, and I had a business manager out in California who was getting 5%, so there was 35% of my salary gone before I even saw it. And, of course, there were taxes to think about, so it wasn't all gravy! I'm just glad I had that business manager (who I was with 40 years!) because he kept everything on an even keel by putting me on an allowance and stashing away all he could. So, in some leaner years later on, I still had the "stash" to fall back on. I actually mailed him every check I got, and he took care of all my bills for all those years. I was lucky in the man I got because there are a lot of horror stories about how business managers took advantage and looted their clients' accounts for their own use. But good ol' Arthur Gage was a big help to me for many years!

There were some changes on the show itself. It was getting pretty expensive to produce, so American Tobacco decided to have a co-sponsor, and we wound up having two of them, each in a different year. The first was Richard Hudnut, with their Quick home permanent kits, and that was a break for the singers and dancers on the show because Hudnut used them in their commercials, a nice source of extra income for them. They also gave products to the gals on the show and were very nice people to have as sponsors.

The next year we had Crosley, at that time a big name in electronics, including TV sets. I remember that well because they gave the stars their choice of several electronic devices, and I was thrilled the day they delivered a brand-new 21-inch (the biggest they made then) TV to our Flushing apartment. A very generous gift, I'd say!

Speaking of gifts, whenever we would go out to do a benefit or a local TV show or any kind of personal appearance, we didn't always get

paid. They would cover all travel and housing expenses, of course, but no cash. However, in lieu of money, there would always be a gift of some sort. I carried home a lot of little "chotckes" from different events, a new 45-record player (these were new at the time and most welcome, especially as I was then recording), little hand radios, writing sets, vases, almost anything you could think of. Our apartment really began to have a "lived-in" look! Some of these shows were a pain in the neck to do and were done for "political" reasons, but others were really great. It depended on who you were working for.

I remember going to Wichita, Kansas, to do, of all things, a rodeo. (I did get paid for this, incidentally!) I was met at the plane by the Junior Chamber of Commerce people who handed me a brand-new, white

Stetson, which I was to wear while I rode around the arena on a beautiful white horse. I had that hat for many years and will always remember that rodeo, for many reasons.

For instance, at the entrance to the arena, there were several burly cowboys sitting up on the fences. They would do the actual contest riding later on but, at the moment, they were just observing and commenting loudly on me in all my finery, with my new hat, getting ready to make the gallop around the arena. They weren't too impressed to say the least! However, drawing on my cowboy movie experience, I managed to make a headlong charge around that arena, waving my hat and shouting my head off. As I came back to the entrance I had slowed enough down to hear one of the cowhands say, "Hey, that son-of-a-bitch can ride!" That was one of the proudest moments of my life!

Being on the road in the summer was fun and led to a lot of unexpected adventures—at once difficult, exciting, fun, sexy—all of which I simply took in my stride!

Chapter 14

Life On the Road

Every summer we had a 13-week hiatus period when the *Hit Parade* was off the air. The timing was great because that was when all the fairs and outdoor shows took place, so, being "available," our agents and managers immediately went to work to book us. Those outdoor shows, plus the nightclubs or supper clubs that stayed open through the summer vacation period, plus the musical tent or dinner theaters, were where we looked to keep busy for that hiatus period. There's an axiom in show business that you have to work while you're hot, and being on a weekly network TV show made you hot and welcome in most of the clubs and venues that had floor shows or vaudeville–type revues. It was always interesting to see what your agent or manager could come up with!

My first summer out I started in Boston at a club called Blinstrub's, run by a wonderful old gentleman named Stanley Blinstrub. Mike, my manager, came with me for my first show but left the next day 'cause he said I didn't need him—a nice compliment, I must say. Actually, I didn't find it hard at all, just enjoyable. The house band was good, I liked the numbers I was doing, and the big crowds we were drawing seemed to like them also, so what more could I ask? Well, maybe one thing: a bodyguard!

On a particular Saturday night we were packed and had a number of long tables adjoining the stage that was filled with older ladies. Now, in South Boston on a Saturday night, almost anything could happen. I was in the middle of my show and it was going very well when I noticed the audience was really carrying on to the point where I was thinking, "Gee, I can't be THAT good!?" It turned out that it wasn't just me.

I had come down toward the end of the stage and, unbeknownst to me, one of the dear old ladies (who was bombed out of her gourd!) had snuck up on the stage behind me and was steadily advancing to GET me! Very fortunately one of the waitresses had seen what was coming and got there in time to save my bacon, or whatever else the old lady had in mind to seize! PHEW! After that I always looked in every direction when I worked!

I also had a fan club in the area (fan clubs were very big in those days, and I had several). This one was run by a great gal named Irene Gaudette (nee Soares), and one night, at my invitation, she brought a number of the members to the show for dinner and the show. They all seemed to have a great time, and it was fun to actually meet all the members, sign autographs, have pics taken with them, etc. Of course I picked up the tab, but at the end of the week when I went to settle up with Mr. Blinstrub he told me that I had no tab! We had done good business and he liked my work, and this was his way of thanking me. A nice introduction to the nightclub business!

A note about fan clubs. They were a phenomenon that sprang up about this time. I had two major ones, one I mentioned above and the other was run by Ruth Joselevitz (nee Goldman) in New York City. She published a club magazine and was very industrious in trying to help my career, for which I was very grateful. And I'm happy to say that, like Irene, Ruth and I are still close to this day.

To continue with my nightclub experiences…Blinstrub's was a wonderful introduction to this life, but the next stop wasn't so great. I was booked into a club called the Copa in Pittsburgh which, apparently, was a place all the record acts played, so Mike had booked me there. After I closed in Boston, I got up early the next morning to catch my plane, got into Pittsburgh, checked into my hotel, and was in the club for rehearsal at three o'clock that afternoon. Phew!

In the club I walked down a long flight of stairs from the street and saw a small dance floor with a small bandstand behind it and some tables out front. On the right side of the club were two huge bars along the wall, one above the other, and I wondered about that. I was to find out why they were there through the week.

Okay, so I met the bandleader, who weighed about 300 pounds and, naturally, was called "Tiny." He turned out to be a wonderful guy and proved it on the first night, which I'll tell you about in a minute.

The band, though small, wasn't bad and we got through the rehearsal in good shape, after which I took my tux and music back to the dressing room. I hasten to add that I was the star of the week, as testified to by my name in lights on the marquee. I mention this only because when I got to the dressing room there was a very pretty gal arranging her makeup and clothes—well, no, not her clothes because it turned out that she was a stripper who was also on the bill!

After my initial shock I politely informed her that I thought this was my dressing room and she had best find some place else, but it turned out that the only other place was a small closet-like room behind the furnace, and she didn't want to go there. So, out I went to ask about this - but before I could get very far, Tiny grabbed me and explained that the gal was the boss' private property and so could dress wherever she wanted to. (I forgot to mention that the club was run by "the boys.") So, I wound up dressing with the gal for the week! Actually, it was kind of fun watching her put on her pasties, etc., so what the hey!

Opening night I did two shows, and then I saw why those two bars were positioned as they were. At the start of the evening all the gals went to one bar and all the guys went to the other, and by the end of the evening they were totally intermixed—a pick-up joint! Oh, well, as long as they came in and liked my singing, what did it matter?!

Earlier, I mentioned that Tiny proved of value to me. It came about in this way. I had done my second show and it had gone very well; LOTS of applause and cheers, and I was feeling very good about everything. However, I was a little punchy because I was very tired with the flying, all the preparation, and the two shows, so I wasn't paying too much attention as I came down off the stage. Before I knew it, I had a female form all over me! She apparently had been waiting for a chance to grab me, and this was it! I really didn't know what to do, but I was trying to fight her off, and not having too much success. Suddenly, Tiny appeared and peeled her off of me and, with a quick aside, told me to get to my dressing room. Which I did.

My roommate had already changed and left, so I was alone in the room, and happy about it. I could change my clothes and take a deep breath and relax a bit. In a moment, Tiny came in and told me about this octopus who had attacked me. She was apparently notorious for this kind of behavior, going for the headliner, and Tiny had been on the lookout for her and so was able to rescue me in good time. I thanked him profusely and headed for my hotel.

But my adventures weren't over, yet. I got back to the hotel, showered and wearily made my way to bed. Now at this time I hadn't been on the road long enough to know that the first thing you should do when you retire for the night is call your hotel operator and tell her to hold all phone calls except for long distance.

Well, sure enough, I had just fallen into a very deep sleep when the phone rang! I managed to answer, thinking it might be Liza in New York, but a very low, quiet, deep, male voice started to talk and, even though I really couldn't hear too much or get my senses together to answer, I finally realized that it was an obscene phone call! By the time I knew what was happening, the operator, who must have been listening in, pulled the plug, and that was the end of that. So I learned to hold calls at night and have done that ever since.

You win a few and you lose a few, but actually, after I got used to the whole thing, it wasn't a bad gig at all. The people couldn't have been nicer. One of the waiters even asked me what I was doing in a joint like this, that I was too classy to be working here. I thanked him and told him I only did what my manager told me to. I even did a freebie local TV show that was produced by my boss. When I complained to Mike about all these things, he just laughed and said that I had to work all kinds of places in this business. Well, anyway, the money was good!

I remember a very nice club in Buffalo, or actually, it was just out of town and only opened in the summertime. The same owner ran a club in town in the winter, but I wasn't available then, so I played his summer club twice, as it turned out. There was a good band and a line of girls, a couple of supporting acts, and the star, who was me when I played there. Such was the power of appearing on a national TV show!

The first summer I was there, Jaye P. Morgan was on the bill with me. She had just had her first couple of hit records and was now getting started in clubs. Turned out to be a very sweet gal and a lot of fun to be around. We used to meet touring around the country at various affairs and still remain friends to this day.

When you traveled around alone, as I did, it got kind of lonesome being on the road, so I used to find a gal to pal around with for the time I was to be there. And I do mean just to pal around with. There was a very young dancer in the line the second year I played the club, and she had "eyes" for me, which I found very flattering. So, between shows, we would have a drink at the bar and talk, and I wound up driving her home after the show. She stayed in a big apartment with two other gals but had her own bedroom so we had some privacy. But I knew she had a boyfriend at home and she WAS very young, so I didn't intend to go any further than a kiss goodnight.

However, the second time I took her home she had other ideas, and as we got to her bedroom she asked me point-blank if I wanted to "bang" her! Being brought up a gentleman (or maybe an idiot!) I said I didn't think it would be a good idea, although I found her very attractive. I knew she was a virgin, and that was another reason I didn't want to go any further. But she took off her clothes, lay down, and again asked me if I wanted to "bang" her! Nervously, I leaned over her, being very careful not to touch anything, and chastely kissed her goodnight...and left! I hope her boyfriend appreciated what I did! I'm sure Liza did!

As a follow-up to that story, she teased me the rest of the week at the club by asking her question again and even coming into my dressing room, sitting on my lap and letting her top fall open. Actually, I'm sure she knew she was "safe" with me and so could fool around any way she wanted with no problem.

At the end of the week, after the last show, I knocked on the door of the girls' dressing room to say goodbye to everyone. Someone called out "just a minute," so I politely waited until the "all clear" sounded—and opened the door to see the line of eight girls all sitting topless at the long dressing table, but with their forefingers carefully placed over their nipples! I managed to suppress a laugh and said my goodbyes, but it was an indelible impression that I carried away with me.

One summer Mike put together a small group: a four-piece band, a girl singer, an emcee-comic, and me to head the bill. We toured around New England at outdoor venues, mostly, and it was an easy gig because we didn't have to rehearse at every stop. I drove my own car and met the group at the date as I had the schedule with me and knew the places and times I was to be there. We were in New Hampshire and had a late afternoon gig at an outdoor fairground. I was supposed to be there, dressed and ready to go, about four o'clock, so had been driving leisurely as we had plenty of time until I got to the hotel. When I arrived, there was immediate chaos.

Apparently a storm was approaching and they wanted to get the show in before it hit, so I was to get there as soon as I could. I quickly checked in, changed into my tux and raincoat and left for the fairgrounds.

My gal singer was Jill Corey, a TV name in her own right, and she was already there, as were the rest of the performers.

The sky was getting darker and darker, so they started the show as soon as I got there, but not before it started to rain—not too hard at first, but hard enough to notice. There was a little roof over one part of our stage and the band was under that so the drums wouldn't be completely ruined. Jill and I, in our coats, were under the roof until we had to work, so after Jill went out in her coat and did her songs, and after a few jokes from the emcee, it was my turn.

I had noticed that we had a big grandstand full of people all sitting in the rain with no covering over them, and no one had left, so I decided to show off. As I was introduced, the rain started coming down harder, so I walked out to the mike (to very nice applause, I might add), greeted every-one, and then said, "If you nice folks can sit in the rain and wait for the show, I can at least join you," at which point I took off my coat and stood there in my brand-new tux! The roar that went up was well worth the clean-ing bill! I think I could have gotten elected mayor at that moment—ha!

Another funny incident happened just outside of Kansas City at a big lake resort. There was a large clubhouse in which we were to do our show and on the bill with me was Connie Boswell of the famous Boswell sisters, now working from a wheelchair but singing beautifully, and a gal trombon-ist, of all things. Her name was Lillian Briggs, very pretty, and she played that trombone like crazy! So, we were a varied group to say the least!

When it came my turn to work, I did my usual opening and first few songs until it came time to take the mike off the stand and wander through the audience singing "I've Got a Crush on You." There was a big crowd, including a number of youngsters, as this was a matinee "family" show. So wandering and singing, I finally came upon a very young lady seated on the floor. She was maybe four years old and cute as a button.

So I got on my knees in front of her and sang as romantically as I could. As I sang, I watched her get more and more inwardly excited until she couldn't stand it any longer and, rising to her feet, she slapped me right in the face! I, of course, reacted by falling over backwards and stretch-ing out flat on the floor which brought the house down. I don't know what possessed the little gal, but I'm glad she did what she did. I wanted to keep it in my act!

Once I was playing Eddy's, a big nightclub in Kansas City, on the bill with the DeJohn Sisters, another act from my manager's stable whom

I have mentioned before. We were in for two weeks and had a very good reaction from the press and the audiences. One night, between shows, I was introduced to several people and thought nothing of it as that happened every night, but this was to have unusual results.

The next night I was in my hotel room preparing for the show and had ordered dinner from room service. So I'm standing in my shorts shaving when a knock came on the door and, thinking it was room service, I reached around the corner and opened the door to let him in and came face-to-face with a young lady (?) I had met the night before. I hastily grabbed a towel and told her I was in a hurry, but she said she had just come up to say "hi" and would have a cup of coffee with me. I tried to discourage her, but just then the room service did arrive and she came in with it. I put on my robe and went out to eat my dinner and again tried to get her to leave, but, finally, I gave her my coffee, finished my dinner, and went back in the bathroom to put on my tux for the evening.

When I came out into the room, she was lying on my bed absolutely NUDE with her arms stretched out invitingly! I quickly told her I had no time for this right now and wasn't interested anyway. (I was, but not with her!) She tried her best to persuade me, to no avail, and I was late for my show, I left her there and told her to be gone by the time I got back.

Well, she wasn't. I got home after two shows and was pretty tired and there she still was! However, she did have some clothes on at this point, which helped. I again tried to persuade her to leave, but no way was she going to, so, finally, I got ready for bed and told her she would have to sleep OUTSIDE of the covers and at the foot of the bed, which, if you will believe, she did! I never laid a glove on her!

The next morning I left bright and early and told her to be gone by the time I got back, and, fortunately, this time she was. I almost hate to tell this story because it sounds so ridiculous, but I swear as I sit here, it's true!

There was a type of gal who sought out the stars appearing in their towns and tried to go to bed with them so they could brag to their friends the next day: "Guess who I banged last night?" We used to call them a very rude term: "starfuckers." They were the ones who became "groupies" in later years. I just hasten to add one more thing. I had my share of young ladies as the years went on, but they were of my own choice. After all, how did I know where my little SF had been, or with whom?!

One other unit I went out with toured Pennsylvania for three weeks. We worked in older towns that had been almost abandoned, or, at least, that was the feeling you got upon arriving there. In one such town, we played an old movie/ex-vaudeville house that hadn't had a live act in it for years. The dust was really like a blanket, and it hadn't been cleaned for our appearances, either.

In our unit was Zippy, the chimpanzee, a very talented, funny monkey—that is, on stage. Offstage was another matter! A young couple had devoted their lives to touring with Zippy and making a very good living with him. They had an old Cadillac car in which they had made the back seat into a large pen for the monk, and this was how they traveled. He was like their "baby" and demanded far more attention than any real baby would have.

Their way of disciplining him was unique. If he did something that he knew was wrong, the young man would pick him up and throw him against a wall! Great confusion and screaming went on and the monk would retreat to the car and sulk until they made up. One thing they had to be very careful about was who they allowed to come backstage. If, for instance, a lady came back who was having her period, it would drive Zippy crazy and he became very hard to control. So, embarrassing or not, they had to check all female visitors. Such was life with a talented monkey!

Well, enough of life on the road…Back to some of my personal problems.

Chapter 15
Can't Win 'Em All

Earlier, I mentioned my philosophy about life giving-and-taking at the same time. Just about the time you get to feeling pretty good about things something comes along to change everything, and, of course, it works both ways. If you're down, boom, up you come, and vice versa. I had begun to feel much better about my whole situation on the show and had a number of outside jobs, so professionally, things looked fine. However, just about that time things at home began to unravel.

Liza had worked her whole life and had done very well until the sad episodes on the Kay Kyser show and the being chased around the casting couch by several producers, writers, and various other types. That had really taken its toll on her. Now she had chosen not to work anymore, but I'm sure she missed it. Whatever the reason, she had become a different person, and I'm sure that my concentration on my work didn't help either. In any event, whether from frustration, anger, feeling left out, or other emotional upset, I don't know, but she wound up having an affair.

Each Saturday, when I was rehearsing at NBC all day, this gentleman (?) would show up at our apartment and spend the day. He was married, with two kids, and I knew him as a very personable, charming "friend" who used to call me to join him for a late afternoon drink. I would find him with a very pretty girl, and he would then call his wife and tell her that we two were going to dinner and ask me to speak to her to prove it. In effect, I became his "beard." The moment the phone was hung up, he and the girl were gone. So I knew him as a horny "cocksman" of the first order. That was the only thing on his mind, but I truly didn't believe that he would zero in on Liza. Looking back, I should have known

Your Hit Parade

it would eventually happen, but, like most men, I never thought it could happen to ME!

I found out about this contretemps accidentally. She was overwrought and had written her girlfriend in California asking her what to do, and then had left the reply laying open on the kitchen table as though wanting me to find it. I never read her mail, but this time, I did. I sat there waiting for her to come home, not knowing just what to do. When she arrived, she immediately saw me with the open letter, and knowing what it contained, burst into a flood of tears.

No need to describe the scene that followed (interrupted by a phone call from His Nibs!) but, as it was just about the end of the season for the *Hit Parade*, I told her to go out to California to stay with her mother while I thought this out.

She swore to me that she loved me and would never see him again. I must say, he was "Mr. Charm," and I had heard the various lines he used on "his" girls, all of which I told Liza. She was aghast as he had promised to divorce his wife, wed her, and they would live happily ever after, etc., saying that he loved only her and all the other garbage he had developed in the pursuit of his prey. Unfortunately, she was completely taken in by him, for a while at least, and only now realized just what kind of germ he was and was hysterical that she had believed him. In the long run, and you'll see how before the book is done, he ruined her life.

So, off she went to California while I had to finish the TV season, after which I headed for California, too, but for a much happier reason. I had been hired to do a big NBC special called *Svengali and the Blonde* which was to be produced at the NBC Burbank Studios shortly thereafter. It starred Basil Rathbone as Svengali, Carol Channing as the Blonde, me as Little Billy, her lover, and the great Ethel Barrymore as the storyteller. In the cast, also, was the marvelous character actor, Franklin Pangborn, who you will remember as the befuddled hotel clerk or host that he usually played in movies. Of all the stars in the cast, he was the one I asked for an autograph! Unfortunately, shortly after the show, he passed away, but I was happy to have had the chance to meet him.

We had two weeks of rehearsals before doing the live show, and a lot of funny things happened while the show took shape. I was a veteran of live TV by now, so was able to take things in stride, but Carol, bless her heart, hadn't done much, if any, TV and got a bit flustered from time to time. She wore strong glasses (when she remembered to wear them) and could never find anything. Given a brand-new script, she had it in a total mess within a few minutes. She took it apart to find just the scenes she was in, and then lost the proper pages. It became spread out all over the floor where, of course, she couldn't see it at all. So, in the first couple of days of rehearsal, it was a real adventure to get her in the right scene at the right time. Even on the air, at one point, she whispered to me, "Where do we go now?"! But, somehow, with Carol, it was all very endearing and everyone loved her. Including me!

We were rehearsing out in Burbank at NBC, and Liza and her mom wanted to come to some of the rehearsals and, certainly, the show. I was still very ambivalent about how I felt and reluctantly arranged for them to be around at times, and did get them tickets for the show. I tried not to think about our personal problems so I could concentrate on my job at hand, but it was a little difficult with the constant phone calls.

However, in spite of everything, I managed to enjoy the rehearsals and the show. It had original music and, I thought, a good script. Everyone knows the exciting Svengali story, full of evil intentions, naive love, broken hearts, and all those other good things that make a fine story. However, when we did the show, even with the superb cast, some of the critics panned us (though I have to modestly say that I got some great notices!) and the show was not a big success. There's an old show business axiom that if you are a hit in an unsuccessful show, nobody cares to remember how good you were. And that was the case with me. I had hoped this might be a big stepping-stone for me, but, alas, not so. So, I read my good notices, sighed, and put them aside.

After the show, Liza, her mom and I went out for a bite to eat. Mom, conveniently, had to leave, so Liza and I were left alone together. I still didn't feel like reconciling, so despite her many tears and protestations, I took her home and left. I had to leave in two days for a nightclub appearance and was very happy to get out of town, feeling it best to leave the situation as it was for the nonce.

I was doing a return gig at the little nightclub in Charleston, South Carolina, and it went very well. However, I received several tear-stained letters and a nightly phone call from Liza which made me think long and hard about the problem. Finally, I decided that everyone is entitled to one mistake, and to let it all blow over, and have Liza fly to Charleston and we would try to pick up the pieces. I was feeling very noble and forgiving (what an idiot!) when she arrived and did my best, as she did, to act like nothing happened. So, I finished my date with the club and we returned to New York.

But something HAD happened and, like it or not, it just wasn't the same. It took about three more years before we had to admit that something important had gone out of our relationship and we must give it up. However, in those years a lot of things happened, both good and bad...the times they were a-changing!

One of the GOOD times happened the next summer when we went out to Hollywood for the hiatus period and I called my old agent, Gus, just to say "hello." He immediately asked me if I wanted to do a movie which, of course, I did! So, he sent me out to Warners (my former home studio) to see the producer and director and, finally, make a test. The part was to run for four weeks and would just fit in with my schedule. And, yes, I got the part! The movie was *By the Light of the Silvery Moon* with Doris Day and Gordon MacRae and was to be directed by an old-time comedy director, David Butler. So, happily, I went through all the preliminaries—wardrobe fittings, publicity photos, script changes, et al, and then had my first shooting call.

I played a "nerd" in the movie, but it was fun part to do. My name was Chester Finley in the script, but Leon Ames, who played Doris' father, got a great kick out of calling me Fester Chinley, and it caught on, so I was that for the run of the shoot. Doris Day, incidentally, was one of the nicest people I have ever met.

Fortunately, I have been very lucky in the people that I have worked with through my entire career. Only a couple of people ever disappointed me. One was David Janssen when I appeared in an episode of his last series, and I don't think he even knew he was being unpleasant. I heard later that he was ill and maybe that was the reason it seemed that he just couldn't be bothered with the little people—like his mind was a million miles away. The whole week I worked with him we never actually spoke face to face—just did the lines from the script. But I was working, so what the hell!

Now, *Silvery Moon* was a happy set, even though there was a minor irritation (to me). It was Gordon's habit of coming in a bit later than anyone else in the morning. We would all be dressed, made up and sipping coffee on the set, and in would come Gordon, with a coat swung over his shoulders and singing his loudest (in that great voice of his), and, with a final swagger, he would say, "Well, let's get this turkey on the road!" Of course, we had been ready for some time, but now we would officially get going! I was very happy when they shot the scene where he and I had a fight in the men's locker room and, much to everyone's surprise (including mine!), I prevailed by knocking him down. Made up for some of those morning starts!

After shooting a couple of weeks, I came across a real shocker while fooling around the set one day. The assistant director always has a scheduling book spread out on his table with the number of weeks the pic is to shoot (in this case, 14) and the listing of each character with the number of those weeks he will work. Remember that my original contract called for four weeks but as I was idly reading the schedule, I was astounded to find Chester listed for all 14 weeks of the picture! Ordinarily that would be a wonderful discovery for an actor, but as I had to get back to New York for the *Hit Parade* on a certain date, I was quite disturbed, as you may well imagine!

'Hit Parade' Stars

I, of course, went immediately to the AD and told him about it, he went to the director who went to the producer, and on up the line. I got paged by the head office and was told I had better call New York to see if they would let me off for the first few weeks of the season. I said I would see what I could do and asked where there was a phone I could use but was told I couldn't use a Warner Bros. phone but would have to find a pay phone!

Angered, I replied that it was their goof, as my contract was for four weeks, and if they didn't want me to call I would just leave when my contact was up. That did it! I was allowed to use the phone in the casting office and American Tobacco was nice enough to let me off for three weeks, and Dave Butler, the director of the pic, offered to do some shots in "limbo" so that I could leave early, and that's the way it was resolved.

I did miss the first three *HP* shows that year, but it was worth it to finish the picture. I'm glad it did because I often see this particular movie on "old-time" move channels and enjoy it over and over again. Incidentally, David asked me if I would be available for his next picture which was to be *Calamity Jane*, also starring Doris, but most reluctantly, I had to turn him down. But I did do two more years on the *Hit Parade* after that, so I guess I made the right decision.

I was glad to get back to the *HP* for the fourth week of the season, and everyone (except, maybe, Snooky, ha!) seemed happy to have me back. So, life quickly settled into a regular routine, and I got to do more of the show than I had before. I was now a full-fledged member of the four-star cast. However, there was an ominous shadow appearing on the horizon in the music business.

Each week the tobacco people had a for-real survey taken of the music played on jukeboxes, on the air, records sold, etc. and that was what appeared on the show. For instance, we could be fairly sure that if Perry Como had a new record and sang it on his TV show, we would have it on our survey the next week. I tried to get him to sing my "Cinco Robles" on his show as it was number eight on our survey. That would surely have put it on our show, but he had just recorded a little Spanish waltz called "Mi Casa, Su Casa" and felt it was too similar to my song and so he wouldn't do it! Mine never got higher than #8…rats! So, the survey was all-important to our show.

And then, along came Mr. Presley! Now I know I'm swimming upstream when I say this, but I was never a great fan of his and wasn't too happy with this turn of events. For now, instead of singing songs from Broadway shows or some of the great composers like Johnny Mercer, Irving Berlin, Jule Styne, et al., we found the survey full of Presley hits and other early-Rock from the three-chord marvels for whom the lyrics consisted mostly of "baby."

In their place, perhaps, they were okay, but on the *Hit Parade* as a listing of America's taste in popular music, well, that was something else. I never understood this phenomenon, maybe it was the utter simplicity of the songs the rockers sang or Elvis' swinging his hips, but there it was. And so, in my mind, and factually, began the decline of the show. At first they were able to put in enough extras and special tunes to alleviate some of the junk, but it couldn't last. And, finally, neither could the show.

Chapter 16
End of an Era

The Hit Parade had been a staple of radio for many years before it turned to television. I remember that, as a teen, I would write down the top ten songs each week, just as a matter of interest, never dreaming that some day I would be singing on the TV show! I still have a couple of the lists written on the backs of envelopes including such songs as "June in January," "Love in Bloom," and "Moon Over Miami."

The transition to TV went very smoothly because the song list was full of hummable, romantic, and exciting songs with, of course, the occasional "novelty" such as "Mairzy Doats" or "The Dipsy Doodle" to provide a chuckle or two. But once rock 'n roll really caught on, it was just a matter of time before the show would fold. I mean, how can you make a survey each week consisting of such things as "All Shook Up," "Blue Suede Shoes," "Hound Dog," or "Purple People Eater"?!

During the 1958 season (our last), I was quietly approached by at least three people to tell me of the future plans for the show. This was all voluntary on their part, and I was very surprised at what they were telling me. In different, roundabout ways, they were saying that the plan was to fire the other three people and to build a new show around me! This was the talk by the production people, and even the tobacco people. Having been treated in a "second class" way for so long, I found it hard to believe, but was secretly delighted at what they were saying!

So, when the end of the season was approaching, we were each told to report to the tobacco office downtown for a talk with the liaison man, the one who had been assigned the dirty work of firing us, for that is exactly what happened. I went in on Monday morning expecting to be told officially the good news that I was going to be retained as per all the whisperings in previous weeks, but, alas, it was not to be.

The tobacco man behind the desk told me that we were all being fired, and then went on to explain that the feeling was that the people on the show were not that important but the survey, the number one song, and the way the numbers were staged were the reasons the show had been so successful. I couldn't believe what I was hearing—people not important! Once I heard that I knew it was just a matter of time until the whole thing folded, and that is exactly what happened.

We four finished out the year, and that was the end of that. They did put on a brave face and hire four people to replace us for the next season, but the public resentment at our summary firing was so great that the ratings dropped by half, and if the tobacco company's pride hadn't been involved, they would have cancelled the show about halfway through the season. As it was, they did cancel the show at the end of the season and took their lumps, brave face and all!

Incidentally, I was called in by one of the tobacco people later on and told what had happened to me. At a meeting "downtown" the list of recommendations for the new year had been passed around and okayed until it got to the president's hands. He dutifully checked everything off until he got to the recommendation that I be kept and skipped over that one. Later came the pronouncement that "if we are going to get rid of three of them, we might as well get rid of all of them," followed by the famous remark that "people are not that important." In other words, he felt that you could use anyone and have a successful show with the survey, number one song, etc. It was extremely cold comfort to me when he was proved so wrong.

In one way I was happy that I would get to go back to California and try to pick up my movie career. So, it was with rather mixed feelings that our season came to an end. We were each given a silver cigarette box (which my wife now uses for jewelry) as a "going away" present, and there were a few tears shed among the cast because we had been together for so many seasons. But, strangely enough, it wasn't the big, tragic farewell scene that one might expect. Maybe we all knew that show business was totally unpredictable and so accepted whatever came along. You did your best and if that no longer worked, you got busy and went on to something else.

A couple of good things happened before the end of our season. I had my hit record, "Cinco Robles," going and on the strength of that was able to get a few guest shots on various TV shows. I guess the most fun was to actually be on the *Ed Sullivan Show*. He had a group of hit songs with their singers, and I was one of those. No banter with Ed; just sang my song, but it was a kick, anyway.

I also did a shot with Patti Page on her show, and that was great. She was so very nice, and I got to sing a duet with her as well as a couple of things on my own. And Jonathan Winters also had a show on which I appeared, again singing "Cinco." I also did a guest shot on Gale Storm's show, playing a guitar and singing. Also, my summer dates were piling up, so the news wasn't all bad.

However, even with all the activity, I was still kind of "all shook up," to borrow a phrase, and I had to do a lot of thinking about the future. But, being young and healthy, I figured that everything would work out all right. In the long run, it did!

Liza and I had to take care of a lot of logistical housekeeping. After all, I had been in New York for ten years and we had been married most of that time, and I'm sure you all know how much "stuff" you can collect in that amount of time! So, we had to consolidate all that, renegotiate the lease on our new apartment (and they were very glad to get it back!), sell some things, and do all the usual mishmash that a big move entails.

Incidentally, the building we lived in was brand new, and the rent was very reasonable, so, on looking back, we might have done well to retain the lease, considering what rents are in New York today! So, we flew out west, without looking back, and hoped that the six years on the *Hit Parade* would provide enough momentum to keep my career going smoothly. Actually, it worked both ways...I was recognized both in and out of the business, but when I went up for an acting part, many times I got dismissed with, "Oh, yes, you're that singer fella!"

Fortunately, there were enough "old hands" in the casting and production departments who still remembered me from my acting days, so that helped. After we found an apartment where we would stay while we looked for a house, I got down to the business of restarting my acting career. Most unfortunately, my old agent (and by far the best one I ever had!) had died and I had to find another who remembered me as an actor. However, I did have the nightclub singing to fall back on, so that tided us over for a while.

I had a three-week date at the Sheraton Hotel in downtown L.A., and during this gig we found a house we liked. As part of my deal at the Sheraton, I was given a suite, so we were staying in the hotel when the phone rang one morning. It was from the painter I had hired to redo the house while I finished my job, and it was bad news. The water heater had burst! Like many California houses, it had been built on a cement slab, so the water had spread over half the house and buckled the hardwood flooring. My painter friend had pulled up a lot of carpet and had it spread out over the lawn to dry, but the hardwood flooring was another matter.

So we piled into the car and drove up to Little Bel Air on Roscomare Road, where the house was situated, to see what we could do. First, we had to let everything dry out and then called a floor man, a plumber, and a carpet cleaner. By the time I finished my last two weeks at the Sheraton, order had been restored and we were able to move into the house in pretty good shape.

Well, the house was in pretty good shape, but my bank account sure wasn't. Like in New York, I couldn't just call the super and get things fixed! This was the first of three houses I subsequently owned, and, as all you homeowners know, something is always going wrong so that, over time, you get to know your service people pretty well!

Strangely enough, as I was a native Californian, there was quite a culture shock upon moving back "home." Ten years in New York was an indoctrination into a whole different way of life, doing everything at double-time and living in the heart of a big city. In L.A. the pace was much slower and when living in a house, you had the yard to think about, as well as personally taking care of things like the plumbing, the electricity, and all the little things that need constant attention. It wasn't long before I was knee-deep in house chores. Fortunately, I am what they call "handy" and so was able to do most of those things, and the other things I just had to learn as I went along.

Again, culture shock! No longer could I simply pick up the phone and have things done for me—now I had to do it! Guess I had been spoiled by apartment living in a big city! We just had to balance the advantages of living in a house with the extra work it entailed. All in all, we did feel it was worth it, except for...oh, well, I'd better shut up about it 'cause I'm sure I'm not getting any sympathy from those of you who have been through similar problems.

Chapter 17
Life Goes On

Life got very busy as we settled down to living the California way again. In addition to setting up the house, I had to look very hard for work, and that meant in a lot of different fields. I could act, sing, emcee, narrate, and practically anything else I might be asked to do, but that meant keeping current in all those fields. So I was on the phone a lot. And, fortunately, I did work in all those fields as time went by.

Guess I'll start with the TV work 'cause there was quite a bit of that. I did get the reaction from casting people that I mentioned before —"oh, yes, you're that singer!" But there were enough of them who remembered me from my acting days so I was able to get TV work.

I did episodes of *Rawhide, Have Gun-Will Travel, Perry Mason, Marcus Welby, M.D., Gunsmoke, Diff'rent Strokes, The Incredible Hulk*, and many others. And, as I did some of these shows and was seen by the newer casting folks, it became a bit easier for me to be accepted as an actor.

When I did *Gunsmoke*, I played a bad guy—the episode was called "Bad Sheriff" (me!)—and I had a gunfight with Jim Arness, who was quite a large man; so big, in fact, that the director decided to arrange the camera angle to make me look a bit bigger. I was put up front near the camera and Jim was put down a slope and they shot over my shoulder which made it look a bit more plausible!

On the first day of rehearsal. as we all sat around a table to read the script, I found myself sitting between Jim and our director, Andy McLaglen, who is also a very big man. It was all right as we sat reading, but when we finished and got up to leave I felt like I was in the Grand Canyon, looking up at these huge men! Fortunately, they were both very nice guys, as was the whole cast, so though I got ribbed a bit about my size as compared to Jim and Andy, the show was great fun to do. I even got to make a pitch for Kitty in her saloon!

At the end of the episode, Arness and I had a gunfight in which I was to be seriously wounded, thus ending the picture, but I kept outdrawing him, and that just wouldn't do. The scene was played in his office and he was seated, and that was the reason for his slower draw. So I had to fumble a bit in order to get shot—which I finally managed to do. Secretly, of course, I was kind of proud that I outdrew him, no matter *what* the reason!

I got cast in a *Have Gun* episode that was to be shot out on location. They did four episodes in a row up in the mountains of the Lone Pine area, a favorite place for location work for Westerns. Really beautiful country, clear blue sky, lots of big trees, a winding stream, all added up to the perfect background for "cowboys and Indians."

As it happened, the episode I was in was the fourth of the series, so I had to drive up at the end of their shooting schedule. My friend, Tony Caruso, a very well-known character actor, was in the same episode, so we drove up together, arriving at about four o'clock at the motel where the company was quartered.

They rushed us into makeup because out on location they were just setting up the first scene we were both in. So, we hurried to get ready and were rushed out to the location where they were shooting. We were greeted warmly and quickly got into our places in the scene where the lighting and camera people had set everything up. I was glad I had memorized my part before coming up to Lone Pine!

Just as we were all ready, there came the call from the assistant director: "Okay, that's a wrap for today, same shot in the morning." So all our rushing was for naught; oh, well, 'twas ever thus in the movie business! So now we all headed back to the motel and, possibly, a drink, and then dinner.

The motel was set up in a courtyard style with all the bungalows facing inward, so everyone gathered on their porches and hollered over at each other to make plans for dinner, etc. As they had been there for three weeks already, they had their favorite places, so it was decided where to go, but not before a bottle of vodka had been produced and everyone who wanted one was given a drink. I did want one as my day had been quite hectic with all the rushing to get up there, get ready and then not to work!

So, while I took off my makeup, I had my drink and then went outside to see what was happening. Richard Boone was the star, of course, and was therefore the leader of the group. He asked me to ride with him in his Rolls-Royce, and off the dinner caravan went.

The restaurant was on the side of a hill with a beautiful view of the forest, and we all piled into the bar to wait for a big table. Before I knew it, one of the cast members who played the guitar was hard at it, and playing very well, I might add. Then I was asked to sing and pretty soon we had a songfest going and everyone was happy as could be. Someone kept handing me drinks, and I was singing with a drink in each hand and having a whale of a time. I had no idea of what time it was, and cared less. We just kept singing and drinking until the waiter came over and said they were closing—it was 1:00 a.m.! So, I never did get any dinner that night.

We did manage to get back to the motel, and I was told I had a 6:00 a.m. call the next morning—or, rather, that morning. I have to say that I was more than a bit bombed, but very happy about the whole thing. However, when I lay down to try to sleep, the bed kept spinning around for some reason and I didn't get too much rest.

Fortunately, the character I played in this episode was a captain in the Army who had been cashiered because he caught another officer messing with his wife, had shot him, then had taken her with him and headed for far places. He also took a bottle of whiskey with him at all times, so my being a little hung over the next day didn't matter too much. However, getting up after about two hours of "rest" wasn't an easy matter, and I did a lot of groaning when the knock came on the door!

But the air was so beautifully clear and cold that it helped me to get going. Several cups of coffee also helped. So, after being made up and driven out to location, I was feeling reasonably human. However, I guess I didn't look as good as I thought maybe I did. One of the ADs took one look and hauled me over to the doctor on the set and told him to "fix this guy up before he collapses."

I really didn't feel that bad, but happily took whatever it was the doc gave me: several pills. What they were I don't know to this day, but they sure did the trick, and I was able to work a full day without any problems. But I made sure I had dinner that night! Such was life on location, and I did have a great week on the pic, at the end of which time Tony and I drove back down to Hollywood in his little MG and arrived safely home.

One other incident which sticks in my mind happened while I was doing a *Have Gun*. The "heavy" was played by a New York actor who employed the "method" style for his performance, the style which strives for actual reality by using sense memory and other mental devices to dredge up emotions. I must admit that, personally, I think a lot of the effort is needless. At least, it is for me. Anyway, we ended up having a fight (in the script) which was the climax to the storyline.

All went well through rehearsals, and the scene looked pretty good. I had had some experience doing "fights" in various pictures and knew how to "take" a punch so as to make it look real. That, and the angle from which they shoot, is the secret for making fights look real on the screen, and we had it all worked out. So on "action" from the director we got into it. It wasn't long before we got to the end which was supposed to be when he hit me and I went down, thus ending the whole affair. Well, he DID hit me, and I DID go down! He got carried away with his method acting, and I suffered the consequences. To say I was mad is putting it mildly, but fortunately no permanent damage was done. It sure ended the scene on a real note, however!

I have talked with a number of stunt men, the guys who do the real fighting in the long shots, and they are always leery of working with the actors for the close-ups because, like this guy, they are liable to get carried away in their pursuit of reality. I saw a stunt man get run over by an actor on a horse in an episode of *Rawhide* because the actor forgot himself in the scene. That could have been disastrous!

I thoroughly enjoyed working in episodes of various TV series, Westerns, drawing-room comedies, musicals, or whatever. Each one was an adventure because of the different contents of the scripts, the personalities of other actors, the way different directors worked, and the intangibles of stepping into a group who had been working together for a long while and were used to each other. You, of course, as an outsider, had to make the adjustments, not them. So it kept you on your toes and thinking very hard!

I have to say that the majority of companies I worked with were very thoughtful in this regard. Another old saying: "the bigger the star, the nicer they are." That usually proved true. To name a few of the nice ones: Robert Young, Richard Boone, James Cagney, Bette Davis, Ann Sheridan, Gene Autry, Doris Day, Raymond Burr, and I could go on and on. Come to think of it—what a great group of stars I had the privilege of working with!

Chapter 18

Ups and Downs

Liza and I lived in our house on the hill and tried to get our lives back together from the effects of the move to Hollywood and the personal problems we were having. I, of course, was worrying about getting new work, and she was fighting a battle within herself about the terrible wrong she had inflicted on me. I have to say that we both tried very hard to make a go of it, but something was missing, something essential.

Much as I wanted to ignore the whole thing, I would find myself feeling "put upon," and then hating myself for feeling that way. She would burst into tears upon the slightest provocation, and as much as we both pretended, it just wasn't working. We talked a lot together, and finally she agreed to see a psychiatrist to help her get over this. But then I made what turned out to be a huge error. I bought her a very fancy cookbook for Christmas. Sounds like nothing much, but she used that book as an outlet for her frustrations and became a gourmet cook.

Again, sounds simple, but as it turned out she would cook these fabulous dishes and almost force-feed me and then wouldn't eat anything herself. Oh, she pretended to eat, but actually would put her bites into her napkin and then dump them in the garbage when she thought I wasn't looking. She even did this when we went out to dinner. Of course, she didn't tell the doctor anything about that. If I had to go out of town for a couple of weeks to do a show, she wouldn't keep her appointments, only canceling them at the last minute so we still had to pay for them! And in the meantime, I was getting fatter and she was getting thinner. All this was symptomatic of an emotional upset of large proportions.

Again, we talked and talked, but in spite of many tears and promises, nothing was settled. It got to me emotionally, too, and began to affect my work until, finally, there was nothing to do but for me to leave. Which I did. I found myself a little apartment and then had to try to get her to move out of the house so we could sell it.

Easier said than done! It took almost three years for me to move her into an apartment and get her to agree to a divorce. That meant I was maintaining two establishments, and I couldn't really do that for long. Finally, with the help of her mother, the agreement was made and I was free. Shaken, but free.

I was having to do a lot of traveling for various jobs, but, at least, it meant that some money was coming in. I had a job for two nights at the Salt Lake Country Club for $1,500, and was very pleased about it, but it turned out to be a bit harder than I had anticipated. The booker up there met me at the plane and drove me to my motel and then attended rehearsals with me and seemed very agreeable all around. That is, until I finished the job.

He gave me $200 cash and a check for the rest which I accepted casually and turned over to Gage (my business manager) upon my return to Hollywood. All well and good, until Gage informed me a couple of days later that the check had bounced!

I had never been "stiffed" before and was stunned. So I called my agent and asked what was going on and was told they would get it for me and not to worry about it.

I then received a personal call from Salt Lake City and the booker was asking me to come up to do another job! He didn't want to go through the agent because it would save him some money. I told him that his check had bounced and I wouldn't go anywhere until that was cleared up. He said not to worry about it as he had the money in his pocket and he'd give it to me when I arrived. (The old "the check's in the mail" dodge). Said he would also give me the plane fare when I arrived.

Needless to say, I got neither. But as long as I was there, I went ahead and did the several jobs he had lined up. But I had learned enough so that as I finished a job I followed him around with my hand out for my share, and that seemed to work. However, I later did several other jobs and he still owes me $600 from the last one. Someone caught up with him, though, because the last I heard he was in a jail. Too bad, because he was an excellent booker and found a lot of jobs. If only he had learned how to handle money! Oh, yes, I finally did get what he owed from that first job—$100 at a time!

My life in musical–comedy got its start about this time and I became a regular song-and-dance man! I had done *Anything Goes* just outside of Chicago on one of my summer breaks from the *Hit Parade*, but now I was free to do shows anytime they were available. I think my next one was *Bye Bye Birdie* at the San Bernardino Civic Light Opera in California. I did three more shows for them in later years, *Bells are Ringing*, *1776* (one of my all-time favorite shows), and *No, No, Nanette* (with the incomparable Martha Raye).

I must tell you a story about Maggie, as her friends called her. She had done the show on Broadway and on the road, so she knew the part very well. Our director-choreographer, Jack Bunch, was excellent and knew Maggie from way back, so, as a result, she didn't rehearse with the group until dress rehearsals. He filled in for her and actually did her songs and all her moves, so we had some idea of where she would be. Watching Jack perform was almost as much fun as doing the show! Toward the end of rehearsals she would lurk in the wings and watch the cast work so as to get an idea of who could handle themselves and who needed help. Finally, we came to opening night never having actually worked with Maggie and not really knowing what to expect—but I quickly learned!

In one scene I was talking with a group of ladies, and Maggie, as the maid, was supposed to tiptoe up to me and whisper something in my ear. She did, indeed, tiptoe up to my ear, but then, instead of whispering, she hollered as loud as she could, an inch from my head! I went with the gag and fell back, stuck my finger in my ear, and stomped around as though in pain. She loved it! From that moment on she knew I could handle myself and showed me no mercy. I never knew what to expect, and it was one of the most enjoyable shows I ever did!

We became fast friends, and with our director friend, Jack, and some others, used to go to her apartment after the show and play poker, which she loved. (She used to drink 100-proof vodka and, after a few belts, would take her teeth out, throw them on the table, and say, "I bet these!") The run of that show was a terrific kick, and I was very sorry to see it end.

Another show I thoroughly enjoyed doing was *Bells are Ringing*, in which I co-starred with the beautiful and talented Anne Jeffreys. This was in Berkeley, California, in their lovely civic auditorium. She was very sweet to work with, had a wonderful singing voice, and it was hard to remember that she was married to the very handsome Robert Sterling. He came to visit her a number of times, though, and there went my fantasies about Annie! How-

Can-Can in Arizona with Patrice Munsel and girl dancer.

ever, that is what they were, only fantasies! I never really intended to make any moves, but a guy can dream, can't he?? I later did an episode of a TV series in which Sterling was starring and so was glad that I had controlled myself!

The first production of *Can-Can* I ever did was in San Francisco at the dinner theater in the beautiful Palace Hotel for the production team of Lewis and Young (or "Screw 'em and Run," as they were known by their actors). The show starred Lilo, the Parisian miss who had been brought straight over from Paris for the Broadway production of the show. She didn't speak English too well and originally learned the part by rote, not knowing exactly what she was saying! But by the time she got to our production she spoke excellent English and with a most charming French accent.

In order to get this part I had to line up with several other actors in a room while Lilo slowly walked down the line to choose whom she wanted to play Aristide. (I thought I detected a slight pause as she came to me but dismissed it as wishful thinking.) Soon she left, we were all dismissed, and the wait was on. My feeling about her pause in front of me was right because a short while later I received a phone call telling me I was THE ONE! Of course I was delighted, and it turned out to be a very lucky break for me because I subsequently repeated the part in four more productions. A good part for me, indeed!

The contract I signed was for four weeks but we did such good business they had to extend the run to 16 weeks. This resulted in a quick negotiation and necessitated a slight raise for me (I emphasize the word "slight"), much to the dismay of the producers. Screw 'em and Run, indeed! But, all in all, it was a very happy production, especially for me, because my father lived in San Francisco, and, though we didn't know it then, he was in the last summer of his life.

He had been forcibly retired after 40 years with Crown Zellerbach Company because of his age, and, after working steadily his entire life, desperately needed something to fill his time. So, he became an official ambassador of good will for the production and spent a lot of time at the box office, made lots of calls to newspapers, came with me on interviews, etc. He also saw the show a number of times.

I mentioned earlier in this book that I had been fairly naive in my youth, and now I know where I got it. Dad was naive until the day he died. An example…

One particular night I had told all the dancers that he would be at the show and to pay as much attention to him as they could as he would be sitting right at stage-side. Well, they did, big time, and he was, to put it mildly, impressed. After the show, when we were having some coffee, he was still starry-eyed and said to me, "You know I think the girls really like me, I mean, *really!*" I assured him they did and were happy whenever he came to see us. Bless his heart! He was a true old-fashioned gentleman.

One night after the show, as we had gathered, as usual, in the Happy Valley bar in the hotel, one of the young dancers approached me and asked why I had never asked her out. I told her I hadn't because I was old enough to be her father, but she told me to let her be the judge of that, so I did ask her out the next night. I suppose she was wise beyond her years because we got along very well, indeed! In fact, we started a relationship that lasted over a year.

Our production in San Francisco ran for 16 weeks and then closed only because Lilo had a contract to appear in the show at the Coconut

Grove of the Ambassador Hotel in Los Angeles. She asked me if I wanted to work with her there, and I told her I would be delighted, and then asked if she could arrange for Joannie, the young dancer, to come with us. She could, and did, and we worked another four weeks in the show down South. It was an entirely different production, and really not as good, but it was great fun all the same. I had an apartment just below the famed strip in Hollywood and all three of us stayed there during the production, a very cozy arrangement.

Another show I enjoyed doing was *Irma la Douce*, the show that became a movie starring Shirley MacLaine and Jack Lemmon. Our production was in Sacramento in Lewis and Young's Music Circus, a big stadium-type theater covered by a huge canvas tent. It was a highly-successful venue and I had played *Redhead* there previously.

In this production I was co-starring with Ruta Lee, and, in one way, this was a very frustrating role for me because the part calls for the male lead to do two roles at once. You are both the young juvenile and older man, and there is even one place where you play the scene with yourself! It was a bit difficult, but, with proper staging and some quick work with a hat and a fake beard, it seemed to work out just fine.

But playing both Oscar and Nestor meant you were on stage most of the time singing, dancing, and acting! Then, after my working very hard, along comes Irma doing a flashy song or dance which garners all the applause; so it was a bit frustrating, I must say! However, I enjoyed all the work. We had a very successful two-week run, and Ruta and I got along famously. She was very pretty, eager, and ambitious—all things I could relate to and I was to work with her again later on.

About two years later the Musical Theater in West Covina was doing a production of *Irma* with Juliet Prowse in the lead role. They had just opened when their leading man, Ron Hussman, came down with the Asian flu which was rampant at the time. I had just finished working in a TV series and was walking in my front door as the phone rang. It was their company manager asking if I would come down and stand by to replace Hussman if he couldn't go on.

Please remember that I hadn't done the part in two years. I told him this, he begged me to do it as otherwise they would have to shut the production down. So, finally, I said I would come down and see the show that night and let them know if I could do it. At that, I rushed down to Covina, picked up the script, and started relearning in a hurry.

A couple of months earlier I had met a dancer, Barbara, in my third production of *Can-Can*, and was getting very serious about her, so serious that she later became my second wife! Anyway, in desperation, I called her and asked her to come down and help me out. Which, bless her heart, she did! She held the book for me and helped me out in the wardrobe department and generally took things in hand while I tried to absorb the show again.

We saw the show and it was apparent that Ron really WAS sick—big time. But he staggered through the show while I made notes, both real and mental, about which aisle he used in which scene and how he had been staged. This production was "in the round" so there was no proscenium, just different aisles leading down to a circular stage on which the show took place. So it was important to know where to enter and exit and which aisle to use for some of the fast changes that had to be made. Finally, and mercifully, the show ended and they took Hussman directly to a hospital, and it was all in my lap!

The director, Miss Prowse, and the other cast members surrounded me and assured me that I could do it, as they would hold a special dress rehearsal for my benefit the next afternoon, and they would all help out in any way they could. So, under a good deal of pressure, I said that I would!

Barb and I went home with the script; I dug out my LP record of the show and went to work. Surprisingly, a lot of things came back to me fairly easily. I stayed up working until at least 4:00 a.m. and then sent Barb home and tried to get some sleep. Getting up at 8:00 a.m., I went back to work and then, about noon, drove down to West Covina to prepare for the rehearsal.

Fortunately, Ron's costumes fit me as we were a similar size, so that was no problem. He had been assigned a dresser to help make the changes in the aisles or wherever they had to be made, so I thought that was no problem. I didn't know until the performance that night that the guy had never been in a theater before and was more interested in ogling the dancers' legs than getting me changed! I had him fired immediately when he wasn't in the proper aisle for one of the changes and had made several other gaffes.

At the rehearsal, I never worked so hard in my life! The songs were okay, as they had come back to me fairly easily, but the staging was another matter as I had to remember which aisle to use as well as the moves on the stage, the dialogue, the songs, and which character I was in which scene! But the cast was very helpful and moved me around the stage when I hesitated.

I'll say they did! In one big dance, or movement actually, I got thrown around by the "mecs," the gangster-type elements who were threatening me. The leader, a big burly type, got a bit carried away and literally threw me across the stage. I tucked under and rolled like a hoop right off the stage, down three steps, and into the front row of seats. Everybody gasped, but I calmly rose, and, still in character, came back on stage and continued. I was so into the learning process that I had hardly noticed! I did notice a few bruises the next day, however!

So we went through the rehearsal and Barb held book while I went through the script again. By that time I was kind of tired and felt I had done about all I could do for a moment, so we went out to have some dinner where a couple of the cast members spotted me and gasped in astonishment that I had taken the time to eat! I just played it "cool" and soon we went back to the theater. Barb had a job that night and couldn't be with me, so I had to rely on the dresser who had been with Ron.

Sure enough! During the performance he was in the wrong place twice for me to change in the aisles and changed me into the wrong costume another time. Needless to say, I was furious and after the show when he was fired, I asked Barb if she would be my dresser for as long as I would be in the show. She readily agreed and never made a mistake for the week I played the part.

One very nice moment occurred at the opening of the show. The lights were dimmed and the announcer's voice boomed out in the dark that, "Mr. Ron Hussman would not be appearing tonight due to illness" and a groan went up from the crowd. However, when he went on to say that "We have been fortunate in obtaining Mr. Russell Arms to take his place," a round of applause broke out which bolstered my confidence no end! I stood there in the dark, said a little prayer, and off we went.

To this day I don't know how I was able to get it together in that short period of time. But I did and then played it for a week before Ron recovered. Management was very grateful and told me to name my price, but all I charged them was my usual price which was $1,000 a week at that time. They also promised that the next show they produced that was right for me, the role would be mine. Unfortunately before that happened, the theater closed down! Oh, well, I guess I proved something anyway.

On the personal side, the experience kind of sealed my feelings for Barb. She had two little girls from her former marriage but at that time it seemed like an added attraction to me, so one evening I asked her to marry me. I think I surprised her and she hesitated a bit and then finally said she'd have to think it over, which she did overnight, and then agreed as to how it would be a good idea.

Chapter 19
Married Life – Part Two

I had bought a small house in Studio City and my buddy, Jack Narz, rented a room from me, so we had what might be called a "bachelor pad" and got along famously. We lived near a great piano bar, so my recreation was nearby, my mortgage was low, I worked enough to pay the expenses, and life was good.

I didn't have any furniture for the house, but we pieced together enough so we could live comfortably until I could buy or borrow more things. And we really didn't need that much—a couple of beds, a stove, a refrigerator, and a couple of chairs, along with a table to eat from. Little by little, I was able to get things together and also got started on painting the place, inside and out. That really kept me busy, so between that and some occasional work, I didn't have time for much else.

An old widowed lady had lived in the house and must have had a friend in the paint business with a lot of vivid pink paint he wanted to get rid of, and he must have sold it all to her because the entire inside of the house was PINK, including the bathtub! So, of course, my first job was to get rid of the color plus some wallpaper in three of the rooms. I knew a painter and was able to borrow a steamer from him to get rid of the wallpaper, but the pink was another matter—just took long, hard hours of scraping, painting and repainting to try to cover that horrible pink. It wasn't going to give up without a fight!

Gradually, however, things began to look better, what with changing a lot of electrical fixtures, the new paint, a lot of donations of odd pieces of furniture from friends, and putting up some new curtains. I was surprised at what I was able to do myself and how much at home I felt. Jack helped when he could but had a TV game show that he was hosting and didn't have much spare time. But we did manage to have some time for r & r, most of which was spent at nearby Whittinghill's Restaurant which boasted a fine piano bar. I got to sing, made a lot of new friends, and because I sang so much I didn't even have to pay for my drinks!

In the previous chapter I mentioned my new gal, Barb. Well, I quickly have to say that all this was happening before I met her, when Jack and I were just carefree bachelors. As the old song says, "We had a lot of livin' to do!" Jack and I went merrily along our way with many social activities.

One that sticks in my mind occurred when a well-known Russian ballet company came to Los Angeles for a performance, as it happened, during the Vietnam War. A prominent attorney in Los Angeles had arranged a party at his home to honor the company, and living in a big, beautiful home on Mulholland Drive, had invited many of his friends to attend. We were invited, or I should say, Jack was invited through his connections at the TV station, where his game show was produced. And he, in turn, invited me to go along.

So, happily, and not knowing any of the details, we proceeded to the big, beautiful home. We were greeted most cordially, our coats taken and a drink immediately thrust upon us. So far, so good. We were fairly early and so were present when the guest of honor arrived. There were two or three ballerinas, a couple of men dancers, and, most important, the director of the ballet and the political advisor of the group.

(Incidentally, I have to mention that the ballerinas, though beautiful, and they were, had a body odor that made it difficult to breathe around them. Apparently, many European women don't believe in deodorant!)

To continue, the party gathered momentum and the drinks flowed, the music played and everyone was having a good time. Then it happened. Everyone was told to gather around and the guests would talk to the group. By the 'guests' I mean the director and, especially, the political director. And how they talked! Right straight down the party line!

My ears started to turn red and I got madder and madder at the things they were saying (the U.S. was using poison gas in Vietnam, etc.) and I started to mutter in anger. Jack was nudging me to be quiet so we wouldn't be thrown out, but I wouldn't be silenced. After a bit more I started to mutter louder and louder and people began to notice me. What made me really mad was not so much what they were saying, but that the so-called American guests were agreeing with gusto.

Finally, some rather large guests began gathering around us and moving closer and closer until one of them suggested that we would be happier somewhere else. I agreed totally, saying that I would be happier ANYWHERE else! At which they started moving us toward the door. I very indignantly said I would like to get my coat and then would vacate the premises on my own, which they allowed me to do. Jack was quiet through the whole thing although he agreed with me heartily. He was simply more discreet than I could be.

So we found ourselves out in the street breathing some fresh air, and I, for one, was happy to be there! Not one of our more successful "parties!"

Another work area opened up for me about this time, as a matter of fact, two of them. One night in the piano bar, after I had finished a set, a gentleman walked up to me and handed me his card. He owned a small company that made film strips for teaching purposes and he needed narration for his films, so he asked me to drop by and talk to him about that. I did so a week or two later, and it was as though he didn't remember anything about our meeting. So, I shrugged it off, dismissed the whole thing, and threw his card in my desk drawer.

However, a few weeks later, when I didn't have a job or any immediate prospects, I went through all the cards in that drawer looking for possibilities of work. My timing was perfect because he had just gotten a new project in-house and was looking for a narrator. So, I went in, did a demo for him and he hired me on the spot. Thus, I added "narration" to my word load. It was strictly industrial narration—that is, for commercial firms, not TV, but fortunately, it went on for several years and led to my working for a number of other clients, so it turned out to be a fortunate meeting in Whittinghill's that night.

The other work area was a bit more exotic—singing and emceeing at both fashion shows and Little Girl pageants. These were to take up a lot of my time and turned out to be great fun, too. I'll have some stories about both in another chapter.

Neither Jack nor I were married at the time, so we had great fun playing the field, from airline hostesses (wonderful!) to friends of friends, to anyone who caught our eye and was available. It kept us pretty busy, I must say. Because of his show, Jack was away a lot and that left me with time and space, and I must admit I took full advantage of the situation. There were a couple of "special" gals but, all in all, I pretty much played it loose - no pun intended!

I did manage to find time to do some TV work, though, in such shows as *Have Gun-Will Travel, Rawhide, Perry Mason*, and several of the popular shows of the time. That was really great and provided enough cash to pay all my current expenses, including the remodeling expenses for the house. I was still hard at work painting and rewiring and adding a new furnace and air-conditioner to the place, so the income was most welcome. All in all, a very busy time in my life!

I had the house in pretty good shape and things running smoothly when I was hired for a production of *Can-Can* at the Melodyland Theater-In-the-Round near Disneyland. I was co-starring with Edie Adams and the great Broadway star, Chita Rivera. What an experience! Chita is dynamite on stage, and in the five productions of the show in which I appeared over the years, no one even approached her performance as Claudine, the lead dancer. Not only was her dancing great, but her acting was just as good. I was fascinated each night watching the enjoyment she seemed to take in that part—a real pleasure to watch and a class act to work with.

Can-Can was a show with a big cast, including a lot of dancers and singers, as well as the featured acting parts. The first scene was in a courtroom where the girls were up on charges of showing too much leg and not wearing any panties (unfortunately, not in our show, but that was the real plot line), and I, playing a very square judge, was in charge of prosecuting them.

Preparing for the opening each night, all those in the first scene gathered in the semi-darkness at the top of aisle eight to walk down en masse to the stage in a blackout, there to set up the action to follow. Just before the show, as we were all gathered, one dancer in particular made the rounds of the actors hugging and kissing and greeting them, except that she avoided me. I stood this for a couple of nights and then stopped her in her rounds and demanded to know why I wasn't included? Without missing a beat, she said she "always cooled it with the stars" and therefore passed me by!

Well, I wasn't about to be left out of the nightly greeting, so I politely asked to be included from then on, and I'm happy to say she complied with my request and that is how I met my Barbara! I found I liked the nightly greeting and asked her out to get to know her better. I found she had two little girls from a previous marriage (Ellen and Julia) and was a working mother. She had been a ballerina with the Ballet Russe and now, aside from appearing in shows, she taught dance.

During the run of the show we kept going out together and it wasn't too long before we found that we really liked each other. From there, in time, it progressed to love and marriage. (Gee, what a good title for a song!) We were married in Malibu, California, by a Justice of the Peace, driven there by my business manager, Arthur, in his Rolls-Royce. Most impressive!

However, there was something I hadn't counted on, and it got a little touchy sometimes when the phone would ring late at night and it would be a former girlfriend wanting to come over! But word finally got around to my various ladies that I was now married and the fun and games were over—for them, at least! Barb didn't like it, of course, but there was no help for it. I breathed a big sigh of relief (and nostalgia, I must admit) when it ended.

Now that I had a built-in family, we needed more room and decided to redo the house. So I contacted an architect I knew, and we wound up adding a master bedroom (from an old garage), a family room and a brand-new kitchen. All that took a couple of months to do and we "camped out," using cots and an electric oven until the great day when it was all competed.

We quickly acquired a dog and a parakeet, Bubba and Opie, respectively, and had great fun with both of them. And so we settled in, got the kids in a nearby school, and felt like a real family. My boarder, Jack, had also gotten married and moved out, so the timing was perfect.

Barb started teaching ballet at a nearby dance academy, and I was doing whatever came along, such as an occasional TV acting job, some narration, and emceeing fashion shows and Little Girl pageants, plus some dinner-theater musicals as they came along, so there was a lot going on. The girls were six and four years old at this time and were not used to a man in the house, so that required some adjustment — on their part *and* mine! We did pretty well for quite a spell, each gal had her own room, and we had the new master bedroom, and so everyone was comfortable.

Barb was a wonderful dancer and performer and I was able to use her in some of my fashion shows. As a matter of fact, at one time we went up to Anchorage, Alaska, for a special being done by the city. Barb danced, did a couple of sketches with me, and I emceed and sang my little heart out. We must have done all right because we ended up going back twice more! Very friendly people up there!

And so, for eight years, we went merrily along until, finally, our bubble burst. The trouble was really between the kids and me, nothing that bears talking about, but it was enough to bring things to a screeching halt. I was away in El Paso, Texas, directing and starring in a production of a murder-mystery, *Catch Me If You Can*, and upon my return I found that Barb had taken the kids and moved into an apartment. I was surprised, but not really. Deep down I had felt it coming on, and so it happened. However, if there is such a thing, it was an amicable divorce and we remain good friends to this day.

So, again, I was a bachelor and vowed never again to marry. But, as we have read, "the plans of mice and men…" proved true for me, as we shall see.

Chapter 20
Fashion Shows and Pageants

At this point in time, 'long about '63 or so, I kept busy in a number of fields; I sang, emceed, narrated, acted, wrote song parodies, did personal appearances at fairs and other outdoor shows, as well as anything else that anyone asked me to and would pay for! But the two venues that kept me busiest were emceeing and singing and writing special material for fashion shows and the Little Girl pageants, especially for the Our Little Miss Pageant that originated in Baton Rouge, Louisiana. But let me start with the fashion shows.

Through some friends I had met a fascinating gal named Dorothy Shreve. At this time she was running a couple of modeling schools and producing some fancy fashion shows. She was one of the first to lace her show with music to complement the beautiful clothes she was showing, and she was looking for a singer to work with her. That, of course, was right up my alley, so I went over to see her and talk about it.

We met in her studio and she asked me to sing for her, a capella, as there was no accompanist handy, which I did. She hired me immediately, but I wanted to do more than just sing. I wanted to emcee the shows, too. Well, she wasn't too sure about that until after the first show I did with her which went so well that she decided to take a chance on the next show and let me emcee.

In addition to emceeing I wrote special lyrics for whatever group we were working with. I would get the name of their president or chairman or whatever and incorporate it in my lyrics, and that was always a big hit. People do love to hear their names and be singled out as special, and I did that whenever possible. I also sang to the models and was able to get romantic whenever the song fit, something I enjoyed very much.

My emceeing was kind of "loose," that is, I made a lot of jokes and even got a bit lewd on occasion, depending on what the dress I was commenting on looked like. Well, not really lewd 'cause I never worked "blue," but maybe a slight bit on the suggestive side. If a very sexy dress showed up, I would say something like, "If my wife ever came home in that I would think I was in the wrong house!" They could interpret that as a crack about my wife or the dress, whichever they preferred.

Every show was an adventure because Dorothy changed her mind so much. We would meet a few days ahead and discuss what we would do— for instance, she would group a lot of green things and I would do an Irish song or if they were featuring cruise clothes in red, white, and blue colors, I would do a sailor song, but always I made the lyrics fit the occasion.

So after our meeting I would go home and try to write some clever lyrics to go with the occasion. Maybe our show was to be at a Saturday luncheon and on Friday night I might get a frantic call from Dorothy saying she couldn't get a particular dress or group of dresses for which I had already written a song, and what could we do? So, after I found a new theme to fit the dresses she could get, I would have to rewrite my songs and save the old ones for the next show. I had quite a collection of song parodies in my portfolio by the time we were through, but usually I was able to use them in subsequent shows. However, many times I found myself finishing up some new lyrics backstage while the show was on! That was hard to do because of all the activity that was taking place.

Because of the very fast pace of the shows I often found myself face to face with a near-nude model as she rushed to make her change of costume, as I was trying to concentrate on the lyrics for the song that I was to sing in the next few minutes. Talk about an ambivalent feeling!

The gals all knew me and we mostly felt like "family" as we did so many shows together, but it was kind of hard for me to remember that when I was staring at a pair of luscious breasts and trying not to notice— unsuccessfully, I might add! However, I never tried to date any of the gals and kept my work separated from my pleasures.

All in all, it was a terrific learning experience for me and stood me in good stead later on in the pageant world. For instance, one year I was hired to emcee and to "help direct" the Miss World USA beauty pageant in Boston, Mass. I was met at the plane, driven to my hotel, taken to lunch, and, finally, taken to the big, beautiful auditorium in which the pageant was to be held.

As the producer and I walked down the aisle toward the stage and where 50 girls were sitting in the front rows of the auditorium, he suddenly turned to me and said, "Okay, Russ, it's all yours!" He then went on to announce in a loud voice that "this is Russell Arms and he will be in charge from now on and you will do as he says!" I stopped dead in my tracks and surveyed the scene of which I was to take charge.

It really was a beautiful, new auditorium but the stage was bare except for a work-light hanging center stage and a very moth-eaten, raggedy-looking backdrop that was hanging askew on the back wall of the stage. This was the first thing I determined to get rid of! The girls all turned to look at me to see who and what they were dealing with, and my mind was racing to come up with something to say.

So, I assumed a confidence that I wasn't feeling and walked on down to greet them with a smile and some banal remarks about how beautiful they all were, etc. However, inside I had become Cecil B. DeMille!

Thinking back to some of the fashion shows I had done with Dorothy, I remembered the red, white, and blue settings we had used with much success and determined that I could use that idea here. So, I started giving orders: "First, remove that backdrop, then get me a lot of colored crepe paper, balloons, and any decorations you came across. I want some platforms brought in and a gas dispenser for the balloons so they will hang in the air. Then, I want the girls separated into two distinct groups, A and B, so we can handle them easier." Anything I could think of that would add to a festive air, I ordered. Then I got the girls on their feet and started moving them around to their proper spots.

I was amazed at how little most of them knew about parading down a runway, so I took a lot of time to show them how to walk and how to say their names properly into the mike and, generally, how to look as feminine and pretty as they could. You should have seen me up there being a model!

I gradually established a bit of order, and a good thing, too, because we were "on" the next evening! We also had an orchestra rehearsal later in the day and I had to cue all the music and pass out my charts as I was to sing during the show as well as emcee.

One another problem was our guest star, Hugh O'Brian, well known as Wyatt Earp on the TV series. He was handsome and charming and a very nice guy, but the stage was not his forte and he quickly asked me for assistance. So, I stood behind a side curtain hidden from the audience.

From there I was able to give him all his cues and tell him what to say when he had to ad lib!

It worked out very well, fortunately, and the show was a big hit, but I really "sweated it out." These girls were, of course, older than the ones I was used to working with, anywhere from 17 to 25, so the atmosphere was very different from when I worked with the little gals. You know, I think I liked working with the little ones the best!

Speaking of the little ones, a funny incident occurred during the Nevada state finals of Our Little Miss Pageant. We were working at the Showboat Hotel in Las Vegas in one of the big ballrooms. They had given me some platforms which we had backed up against curtains on one side of the room and through which the girls would enter, stepping up onto platforms. I had music playing as they entered and it all went very well as we got all of the contestants in their places, ending with a little four-year-old at the very point of the graduated platforms, right in the middle of the ballroom.

The audience, mostly relatives and friends of the girls, was seated on the other side of the room. I turned to them and said how proud they should be as the girls really did make a beautiful sight. Then I turned to sing "Thank Heaven for Little Girls" in tribute to the lovely scene, when out of the corner of my eye I saw the little four-year-old on the edge of the platform hop off and start across the floor toward a door!

I interrupted my song to say to her "where are you going?" At which she drew herself up to her full height (which came up to about my waist) and sounded off in her loudest voice, "I have to go potty!" And, with great dignity and aplomb, off she went. I hasten to add that she did come back just as I was finishing the interrupted song and, with great dignity and aplomb, took her place and casually awaited further developments. I'd like to say that she won the title in her category, but I honestly can't remember if she did or not. She should have gotten an award for nerve!

I wound up working for Our Little Miss for about 15 years and watched a number of the smallies grow up in the pageant system. There has been a lot of criticism about little girl pageants (and some of it deserved), but I found most of the problems began with some overeager mothers. We forestalled that by having a Mothers Meeting the first day and laying down the law about any kind of abuse or overjealous actions. We believed that the girls were winners simply by being there as they all had won several local pageants in order to be invited to the big state one. We instilled this feeling into the mothers and made sure they appreciated their kids as stars at all times. So we had very little, if any, trouble with "stage mothers."

Three other incidents are worth telling, I think. I was doing the Louisiana State Pageant in Baton Rouge one year and we were working with the Our Little Miss, or middle group, ranging in age from 8 to 13. We had gotten to the top ten and were having them model their sports outfits for the final time. I would call their name and they would come out to the center of the runway and stand while I talked about their background and interests after which they would proceed down the runway to give the judges a final look at their work.

Well, one ten-year-old heard her name, came to center stage, and waited while I spoke, but I noticed that she didn't move when her cue came. As I looked over at her she turned to me with a desperate, glazed look, and I knew there was trouble. Without further ado she began to pee—a gusher! Everybody was stricken right along with her, but nobody moved, so I quickly ran to her, put my arm around her, and guided her off stage, all the while hollering to my ladies to get a towel and dry things up. As we got off stage, her mother, who had been in the audience, came running up and took her in her arms, and I had to get back out on stage and smooth things over. So, we proceeded and finished without ever seeing the gal again.

The awards were given and pictures were being taken and congratulations were in order when the mother, carrying her daughter who had her face buried in her mom's shoulder, appeared and stood at the side of the scene. The mom beckoned to me and, when I went over, she asked, "Would you please speak to my girl as she hasn't said a word since the accident happened and now won't even look up from my shoulder."

I gently took the gal's face between my hands and comforted her by saying, "Hey, everyone has accidents and you really should be proud of yourself because you made the top ten, and just think of all the gals who didn't even do that." Well, I continued in that vein for a bit until I finally got through to her and she actually smiled at me. With that, her grateful mom, through her tears, thanked me and the incident was over, though I'm sure it will never really be over for the girl and her mom, and even for me. Some of life's lessons are kind of hard to learn!

At that same pageant we had a "guest star"—she was a four-year-old Queen from the preceding year's young La Petite division who had been invited back to entertain and then was to hand over her crown to the new winner at the appropriate time. She was a little bitty thing but with a huge personality which came out very unselfconsciously when she sang. The incident I'm talking about happened one afternoon in the middle of some competition when the contestants needed to change clothes, etc., so to kill time we had our special guest star sing for the audience.

She was all dressed up in her royal raiment, complete with crown and sash, and came out confidently to the center of the stage to perform. Her song was called "Fantastic," and each time she came to that word she would really lay on it—with a big, swooping shriek!

The first time I heard it I almost fell off my podium, and as it continued, I practically got hysterical, as did the audience. To complete the picture, in the wings, out of the audience's sight, but positioned so her daughter (and I) could see her, was her mother who must have weighed 250 pounds. She was crouched there to coach the child by softly singing along, just loud enough so the daughter might catch any cues she needed.

From where I stood I could see the whole picture, and after Kelli finished her song it was several moments before I could continue. Each time I would try, both I and the audience broke up all over again, absolutely hysterical. Needless to say, we used her and her song several times during the week of the pageant!

The other incident I wanted to mention happened at the California state pageant, one that I had done regularly for several years, and so I had gotten to know some of the girls as they grew up.

One year I was in the lobby of the hotel as the registration was taking place when, all at once, there was a big flurry and a four-year-old who I had worked with the preceding year came running up to me, grabbed me around the leg shouting, "Mr. Arms, Mr. Arms," obviously happy to see me. I patted the top of her head (she came up to just above my knee) and welcomed her when she suddenly looked up and said, "Mr. Arms, you got GIRLS' shoes on!"

I did have tasseled shoes but her amazement really broke me up. Finally, I fixed everything by telling her that my sister had lent them to me! I really did love those kids, and you certainly didn't know what to expect from them.

So, for several years, between the fashion shows and the pageants, I had a wonderful time and got to meet a lot of great people, people I still consider as friends to this day. I was a part of two unusual worlds and am very happy I had those experiences which give me such wonderful memories to savor in my "old age."

Chapter 21
If Only I'daaa

I know a lot of you out there have had the same experience I had many times—having to decide which fork in the road to take—a profound choice that could possibly change your entire life. So, finally, you make your choice, live your life a certain way as a result, only to stop one day and say to yourself, "Gee, if only I'daaa" made the other choice, of course. You think how very different your life could have been and maybe, how much better. Or maybe how much worse! Anyway, I've collected a number of such choices for my own edification and perhaps for your enjoyment. These are a few of my "what might have beens!"

The first one isn't so much my own choice as a decision that was made for me. I had just finished my third major movie in 1942, *Wings for the Eagle*, and was immediately drafted into the Army. A couple of months later, while deep into basic training in the wilds of Camp Crowder, Missouri, I received a package at mail call from my agent which included reviews of that last picture.

One, in particular, stood out to me. It was a column by Louella Parsons. (For those of you who don't remember, she was a formidable columnist for the Hearst papers whose word was law in the movie industry. She could make or break a career, it seemed). In her column, she reviewed *Wings for the Eagle* and was particularly kind to me.

She said something to the effect that I was a "find," a potential "star-leading man" and "there would be a place waiting for me when I got back"…and she went on and on in that vein for about a quarter of her column! The kind of thing that an actor yearns for. And here I was on KP, amidst the pots and pans. The whole thing was alleviated by the fact that we were involved in a big war, and what I was doing was extremely important (not the pots and pans!), but I've often thought of what might have been if only I'daaa...been available!

The last year of the *Hit Parade* was another example of something that might have been. During the rehearsals toward the end of that season I was approached several times by production people all saying the same thing—that at the end of the year everyone was going to be fired except me and the new show would be built around me. I found that hard to believe, but at least three people volunteered that information, and they were people who should have known. So when the chosen day for us to appear "downtown" and be told about our futures came around, I went in with a confident air only to be told that I, too, was going to be axed. So much for advance information! What a difference in my life if only I'daaa...been told the right thing and all that had actually happened!

Back in Hollywood, a casting agent took me out for a part in a syndicated series called *This is Alice*. He had known me before I had become a singer and so he knew I could act. However, the director didn't know that and said he was delighted to meet me but needed an actor for the part.

My casting director friend insisted that I was perfect for the part, but the director was adamant that he wanted "an actor." It took the better part of the afternoon for him to be convinced that I should do the part and, finally, grudgingly, he agreed to cast me. I worked two days later on my first scene which proved to be most interesting: no lines, but lots of drama.

My part was that of a father who had left his family several years before and was now returning, unbeknownst to them. It was Christmas and the family was gathered around a tree in the living room as I approached the house. I was to quietly move up to the window, in the snow, and watch them without being seen. So, I did as directed and reacted with much emotion to seeing my daughter, Alice, and the family, and, finally, turned away to leave. That was the scene and I gave it my all—even to a tear or two in my eye in the big close-up.

The director was very impressed and called me a "thinking actor," which was a big compliment. I finished the three-day shoot and, as I was leaving the set, the director said to me that if the series was picked up they were going to write me into the script as a regular. So I had convinced him, at least. Needless to say, they weren't picked up! If only I'daaa...had this opportunity in a hit show!

On a personal note…Dorothy Collins, my sidekick for six years on the *Hit Parade*, had divorced Raymond Scott and with her two girls had moved out to Hollywood. I didn't know this, but it happened that she was appearing as the guest star on the *Dating Game* TV show and I had been called to be one of the three guys from whom she had to choose, without her knowing it of course. We were hidden behind a curtain, and they had asked me to disguise my voice which I did so well that she wound up choosing one of the other guys! But we had a nice reunion after the show and that led to some dating between us. I had always had very warm feelings for Dorothy who was one of the nicest people every put on this earth.

But the timing couldn't have been worse! I was wooing Barbara (who did become my second wife) and was suddenly caught in the middle of an emotional situation! I harbored the thought of actually asking Dorothy to be

THE SHILOH AGENCY
12444 Victory Blvd., Suite 407
North Hollywood, CA 91606

Russell Arms in the 1970s.

my wife and yet I had fallen in love with Barb, too. So, what to do? Here was the fork in the road and a decision to be made. After much pondering and soul-searching, I finally decided to marry Barb. Was it the right decision? I don't know for sure and have often wondered what my life might have been like if I had asked Dorothy instead. Maybe I'm taking a lot for granted, but I think she would have agreed. So, once again, a fork in the road. Did I do right? I did marry a wonderful gal, but so was Dorothy...If only I'daaa??

As we were finishing shooting *By the Light of the Silvery Moon*, our director took me aside one day and said he would like me to be in his next picture which was to be *Calamity Jane*, again starring Doris Day. I was thrilled but realized the timing was wrong as I had to hurry back to New York to resume the *Hit Parade* show. It was just at the beginning of the season for the show and the thought crossed my mind that I should try to get a release for as long as was needed so I could do the picture.

Which was more important to me and my career: continuing with the TV show, which I had worked so long and so hard to become a part of, or going for a full-time movie career? This was one of those times when you have to take a big gulp of air, close your eyes, and CHOOSE! So, I opted to return to TV and had to thank Dave Butler, and tell him, regretfully, I just couldn't do the film. Again, I have often wondered what my life might have been if I had opted for the movies instead...If Only I'daaa...become a movie star??

I had another, easier, choice toward the end of my Army career. I was stationed at Camp McCoy, Wisconsin, in the dead of winter just about Christmastime. The commanding general, who came up through the ranks, was a very nice man and just happened to have a very nice daughter who was visiting him over the holidays. I was introduced to her and she was intrigued with me, partly because of my Hollywood background, so we began dating. The general would send his car around to the Bachelor Officers Quarters to pick me up (and didn't I get it from my junior officer buddies for that!) for my date with his daughter. Of course, I was the only junior officer at the parties he would give at his house, so I became the "gopher" for all the majors and colonels who were present. This, I didn't mind at all, flexing and fetching drinks for all and sundry, as well as any other chores that came up.

Fortunately, one of the general's favorite things to do was to gather everyone around the piano and sing. I happened to know a thing or two about that and joined in eagerly with the result that we all began to be good friends. He took me in the kitchen one evening and asked if I had

Doris Day and Russ in *By the Light of the Silvery Moon*, 1953.

ever considered making the Army a career. Having spent six years in a military school as a kid and now just completing four years in the Army as an adult, I might easily have said that I had considered it, indeed, but the words just wouldn't come out.

I was much too ready to return to Hollywood and, reflecting on what Louella Parsons had said, to resume what had been a promising career in the movies. So, I told him that I didn't think it was such a good idea for me, but thanked him for his interest. I truly feel that if I had pursued the idea, both the career and the daughter, I might still be in service! If Only I'daaa...thanks, but no thanks!

I was asked to make a pilot film for a half-hour comedy; a test show which, hopefully, would be picked up for a series. It was being done by two young men with little, or no, experience in Hollywood, or even show business for that matter. However, they had financial backing and were really gung-ho about doing this show and were convinced they had a hit situation. I asked for $1,000 per episode, but they would only agree to $750 for the pilot and then, maybe, we would renegotiate for the series. So, I finally agreed and settled down to learn my script.

We shot for a couple of days and, after they saw the "rushes," they called me aside and said they were so pleased with my work that they would give me $1,500 per episode when the show was in production! So, I happily went to work each day, but with increasing misgivings because I could see a number of problems developing.

Anyway, fast-forward and we are in the projection room waiting to see the finished product. They had invited a lot of important people and before the showing both got up and made big speeches to lots of applause and general happy attitudes. Then the lights went down and the show was on! I have to say the "finished product" was, to put it kindly, not very good. Afterwards, when the lights came back up, the room had practically emptied and those who remained quietly slunk out of the room trying to avoid seeing each other. Again, what might have been, If Only I'daaa…been in a good show!

My last story is the most heartbreaking for me. While still in New York, I had a call one day from the Rodgers and Hammerstein office asking me to come in and see them. They were about to make a movie of their great musical, *Oklahoma*, and were looking to cast the picture. I was thrilled to be there, naturally, and we set up a time for me to come to the theater and do an audition.

When the day finally arrived, I went to the theater full of hope and joy and, as I came on the stage, I could dimly see a group of people sitting in the audience gathered around the great R & H themselves as I was told to begin.

I remember that I sang "The Surrey with the Fringe on Top," which had gone very well. Then they asked me to do another, so I sang "People Will Say We're in Love" which, happily, also went very well. After the usual "thank you," I was ushered out of the theater, almost unable to breathe because of the experience. I went home hardly daring to hope that anything would come of it, but the next day the phone rang and it was the R & H office. They wanted me to make a test for the part of Curly!!

A couple of weeks later I was sent out to Hollywood and began preparing for the test which was to be shot at MGM. In a few days, after some rehearsal, I was told to report on a certain Saturday to actually film the scene. Turned out that they were going to shoot four tests that day and I was the last to be done. So I had to hang around all day and, finally, about four o'clock, I was on.

Now remember, it was four o'clock on a Saturday afternoon and

Russell Arms in the 1970s.

they had already done three tests and the crew was tired of the whole thing, so already the bloom was off the rose. However, I gritted my teeth and set to work, I was working with a very nice young lady and we did a scene and sang a song together. I had already sung "Oh, What a Beautiful Morning" alone, and now we sang "People Will Say We're in Love" together and then acted out the rest of the scene. There was a pause and, suddenly, the crew and everyone on the soundstage burst into applause! At that hour of the afternoon and with everybody tired and wanting to go home, they burst into applause!

So, I went back to my rented apartment in a glow and waited. Two days later I got a call from a friend at the studio who told me they had seen the test and liked it very much and that he felt I had a good shot at getting the part! I asked if I could see the test but he said they weren't letting anyone see anything yet, so I hung up and proceeded to wait some more. Another two days and another call from my friend saying the same thing, that I had a very good chance of getting the part. You can imagine how I felt!

Two more days, and another call, but this time it was from the R & H office telling me that I could return to New York! Which I did. One more call from the R & H office there to thank me and that was it. I still don't know what happened except that I didn't play Curly! Oh, my! If Only I'daaa…got the part!

Choices, choices! Some good and some bad, but all have to be made. Whatever, once you choose your path—or it is chosen for you—you have to live with the results. Sometimes it's easy and other times…well, If Only I'daaa…!!!

Chapter 22
Flashbacks

I've always had a problem remembering names—faces I can remember, but names are another matter. Seems to me that everyone should wear a name tag to solve that problem. To be fair, I was at a bit of a disadvantage because I was seen on TV and people thought they knew me personally, and so would come up to me and say, "Hi, Russ," and expect me to answer in kind when I had no idea who they were.

Got a bit embarrassing at times! I've had someone come up to me and say, "Oh, I know you...you're...um...ah...Oh, gee, I know" and, trying to be helpful, I would say, "Russell Arms" only to have them reply, "No, no, that's not it!" Or even worse, someone would come up to me with a big smile and say, "Hey, didn't you used to be Snooky Lanson?" Well, what could I do—just smile and say, "Yes."

I never quite got used to being "famous," or at least, well known. Innately, I was always quite shy and was much happier performing on a stage or in a TV or movie studio than doing the "social" bit. Many times at a cocktail party or such, I would latch onto someone who knew me and would stay with them most of the evening instead of circulating and "playing the room" as I should have done. Many a deal is struck at a social function, but I never got the hang of it and so couldn't use that avenue of advancement.

What I really did enjoy was to work with some old-timers and listen to their stories. Two actors immediately come to mind, the first is John Carradine, who went from Shakespeare to playing slimy villains in some pretty bad "B" movies, but was always fascinating to watch. (I'm sure you remember his three talented sons, David, Keith, and Robert.)

147

Well, I had the pleasure of working with him in a funny play, *Arsenic and Old Lace*, in which he played another of his patented villains.

That was in summer stock in San Diego and was great fun to do. After the show each night we would gather at a local pub and, as long as he had a drink in his hand, John would regale us with wonderful stories about other shows he had done and some of the great stars with whom he had worked. Needless to say, I made sure he always had a drink, and he would continue until closing time. A great experience!

The other actor I recall as a wonderful storyteller was Chill Wills, the scruffy, old Western character actor. I worked with him in a Gene Autry western, *Loaded Pistols*. While there was no drinking involved out on location (or there wasn't supposed to be), Chill just enjoyed himself between takes by gathering a gang around him and holding court. He had the wildest stories to tell that I've ever heard. Some of them were simply old jokes that he personalized, but a lot of his stuff consisted of actual experiences he'd had, embellished just a bit, of course, but fascinating to listen to.

Another flashback. I was hired to play Papa in a funny old Phil Silvers musical, *High Button Shoes*, which was to be done at the wonderful St. Louis Municipal Opera, a huge outdoor theater with about 10,000

Russ with Gene Autry and Barbara Britton in *Loaded Pistols*, 1949.

seats and the biggest stage I've ever seen, even going so far as to have real trees in the middle of the stage which provided a bucolic atmosphere.

Well, I was playing opposite the beautiful and talented Marge Champion, who was married to the brilliant choreographer and dancer, Gower Champion. As Marge and I both lived in Hollywood, we decided to work out a big dance routine we had together ahead of time so we would be ready when we got to St. Louis. There was only a week of rehearsal there, so we wanted to be prepared. We spent about three weeks learning the routine and, please remember, I was not a dancer, per se, just an actor-singer who could hoof a bit.

So I sweated a lot to get the dance down, and Marge, bless her heart, was very helpful and understanding about whatever shortcomings I had. I must say, though, that we finally had a most entertaining routine and I did hold up my end. (And, by the time we finished, it needed holding up...ha!)

So, now we got to St. Louis and went into real rehearsals. The producers were very impressed with what we had done and it was incorporated into the production, and, I must say, I was feeling pretty proud of myself and a bit cocky about what we had accomplished. Then came the blow! Marge told me that Gower was coming in to see the opening! Picture my situation. I was insecure enough about the dancing and now Gower, the world-famous choreographer and dancer-husband of my leading lady, was going to be there to see it!

There's an old showbiz term, "flop sweat," and it certainly applied to me that night. Marge didn't seem a bit concerned and assured me that Gower would love it, but I wasn't comforted. However, the show must go on, so it did. Well, not only did it go well, but following Marge's lead, I ad-libbed a few smart remarks that got laughs, and we did an encore, and it was the hit of the show.

Plus, and a BIG plus it was, Gower loved it! Or, at least, so he said — and he wouldn't lie to me, would he?!! It wasn't too much longer before Gower passed away, much too soon, so I'm glad I had the opportunity to meet him and get to know him, if only slightly.

Early on in my summer stock career I did the wonderful Cole Porter show *Anything Goes*, just outside of Chicago in the Music Theater-in-the-Round. Good cast, too, including Jack Guilford, the very funny New York character actor (now deceased), and a very young Carol Lawrence playing my girlfriend. She was just out of school and lived nearby and wanted desperately to be in show business. We got along very well and I was even invited to her house for dinner during the rehearsal period and enjoyed meeting her family, as well as having a fine Italian dinner.

Now let's fast forward a few years to when I was hired to do a TV show called The *Bell Telephone Hour*. It was a big weekly musical show and usually had three or four guest stars to sing or dance or whatever. The week I was on, I was surprised to find that my old buddy, Carol Lawrence, was also on. So, I really looked forward to rehearsals and seeing her again to catch up on old times.

Now, you must remember that this was after she had her big Broadway success in *West Side Story*, and was now considered a Broadway star by the public and, also, by herself. I was in the rehearsal hall waiting for everything to begin when in she walked, followed by an entourage of "boy" dancers who were to appear with her.

Happily, I walked up to her to say hello and perhaps give her a hug of congratulations (I hadn't seen her since her success), only to be passed by with a frosty, "Oh, hello," which left me standing there with egg on my face. Apparently, I hadn't kept up with her in the stardom race in her opinion, and so wasn't worthy of a proper greeting. It was really a bit of a blow, but, what the hell, things like this happen.

Now let's fast forward again. I'm back in California at the beautiful Crystal Cathedral to do the Christmas show for Dr. Robert Schuller and was what you might consider the "lead" in the show because I was the host and storyteller of the script. And who was playing the Virgin Mary, but Carol!

Our inevitable meeting was very strange. We were like a couple of dogs circling around each other, warily looking for a way to greet each other and knowing there was a bit of baggage between us. We finally got through the meeting and, as I didn't have any scenes with her, everything was all right from then on. I don't really know why all this happened, but it did, for which I'm sorry. I hope Carol reads this and knows that I think she's a wonderful singer and actress and would love to be friends!

Another memory. It was the usual custom for a lot of us to meet at Gage's (my business manager) each night at cocktail hour and catch up on all the gossip of the day and thrash out whatever problems we might have. Among the regulars were Jack Narz (my buddy, the game show host), Warren Stevens (a wonderful actor), and Leslie Nielsen (the wacko comic actor), as well as several others, so there was usually a good group to kibitz with.

Well, one evening we were all gathered and suddenly, in the midst of all the chatter, came the unmistakable sound of a large, juicy fart.

Nobody paid too much attention to it as these things happen, especially among a strictly male group. But then it happened again, and still again, until it couldn't be ignored. We began stirring around and sniffing the air when Leslie broke up and calmly laid a little hand-held toy on the bar which, when squeezed, would make the appropriate sound. He, of course, had been making the sounds and thought it was hilarious that we had all been taken in. He became famous for his "farts" around Hollywood, the kind of humor that subsequently, stood him in good stead in the comic cop pictures that made him famous!

I was playing the Steel Pier in Atlantic City one summer (my second time there) and my co-star was the voluptuous, funny lady, Dagmar, who you will all remember from some late-night shows where she played the "dumb" blonde with all the sex appeal. Dumb like a fox, that lady!

It was, of course, in the summertime, in sultry, hot weather, and we did five or six shows a day, and we stayed pretty much in our dressing rooms waiting to do the next show. Well, Dag's dressing room was just opposite mine and we usually sat with the doors open to catch whatever breath of air there was. Between shows, of course, we took off our "working clothes" and sat, either in a light robe or in our skivvies, until it was time to go to work again.

One hot afternoon there we were, me in my shorts, and across the hall, Dag in just a very light robe. I wouldn't really have noticed too much except that she happened to be in a teasing, devilish mood, and as we would exchange an occasional word or two, she would "accidentally" let her robe fall open slightly and that spectacular figure would be partly exposed to my gaze. She was just kidding around, I know, but it is an indelible memory from the past, and one I cherish!

I remember lots of little incidents, like the county fair we played in upper New York state one fall. There had been an ice show playing there, and when we came in for two nights they simply put some boards down right over the ice for us to use as a stage, and, believe me, on a very chilly fall night it was hard to sing without my teeth chattering. The cold started at my feet and worked its way right up my body until it came out the top of my head! Some of my lyrics must have sounded very strange! Took me an hour to thaw out after the show!

There was the time in a Reno nightclub where I was to open in two days. There were several people, including a famous dance team, a man and his wife, who were just closing their engagement in the club, gathered around a table having a drink. I was seated next to the husband and was appalled to feel his hand under the table groping my leg with sinister intent. Quickly, I excused myself to go the john and when I returned made it very plain I wasn't interested by moving my chair as far away from him as I could get.

In my earlier days in New York I had several incidents with producers or directors of a like nature. Once I was to read for a part in a dramatic road show. The appointment was for 11:00 a.m. in the producer's office, so I thought nothing of it. I arrived and was told to wait for a bit in the outer office and when the secretary told me to go on in, I eagerly opened the door and stepped into the office.

The instant I did I knew I was in the wrong place. The office was very dimly lit, with all the curtains drawn, low music was playing, and I could barely make out a desk in the corner with a dim figure seated behind it. A low, whispery voice invited me in and asked if I was here to read for a part in his show. I hesitated just a second and then told him (I think it was a him) that I thought I was in the wrong place and really didn't want to go out of town in his show, and, without further ado, left.

Another time I had a noon appointment in a producer's apartment. When he answered the door in his robe and obviously nothing else, I knew again that all I wanted to do was leave, which I managed to do without much of an incident.

Everyone always talks about the "casting couch," but it usually applies to a girl being seduced in an office. What do they call it when a guy gets chased around with evil intent?!

On the reverse side of this coin my old agent Gus, told me of the following incident. He was in his office and had an appointment to see a mother and her daughter about possibly representing the daughter for film work. After a bit of conversation the mother instructed her daughter to stand up and remove her long coat, under which she wore nothing! Mom then said that her daughter would do anything Gus wanted if he would represent her! (He never told me what his answer was but, knowing him, I'm sure he was a perfect gentleman.)

Sex was (is?) always a big part of the game…ah, show business!

Chapter 23
Future World

I was more or less satisfied with my life as it was going, but fate has a way of stepping in and changing one's plans. I was living as a bachelor, having sold my house after Barb and the kids left, and I was doing a lot of commercial narrations, an occasional TV spot, and emceeing the Little Girl pageants and doing the fashion shows, keeping busy and paying the bills. I also had a relationship with a very lovely lady and wasn't into the social whirl anymore. So, I guess you could say, I was content.

Just about then my agent called about doing *Can-Can* again. I had done the show four times already and loved doing it but felt that I was getting a bit "long in tooth" to play the part of Aristede, the prudish judge, anymore, so I turned down the offer and thought no more of it. A week went by and the phone rang again, and again the agent told me they wanted me for the part and had upped the salary! I still felt that it wasn't right for me and turned it down a second time. Another week went by and, yes, the agent called a third time about the show. And again, the money was raised!

I was about to flatly, and finally, turn it down when he told me they were using Yvonne DeCarlo, the glamorous movie star, as the leading lady, and so they needed a "mature" leading man to play opposite her. Now it began to make sense to me. I would be fine with Yvonne and the money was good, so I went in to meet everyone and talk about a deal.

It was to be done in Atlantic City at the Tropicana Hotel, would run for four weeks and would be the first Equity show in AC, so, all in all, it seemed like a good move.

None of the cast got their housing paid (except Yvonne), but they had made arrangements with a motel right across the street from the

Tropicana for us to get special rates, and most of the cast moved in there. We wound up calling it "Motel Hell." It was kind of like a boarding house without board, but everyone was there so we did a lot of socializing and the events that went on there would make a book themselves! But, mainly, we were there because it was close to rehearsals and that was the reason we were there.

However, after the first week passed, I felt there was trouble ahead. Having done the show many times before, I could have opened immediately, but they were having a lot of trouble with Yvonne. No one knew what the trouble was, but she just couldn't seem to learn her lines and didn't seem interested in doing the preliminary shows that were lined up before the official opening.

Almost in despair, I waited in a hallway near the rehearsal hall where all the dancers and singers were learning their parts and rehearsing steps while Yvonne was in another room being coached by two or three of our producer-directors. As I sat there one day, the nicest of the six producers happened to walk by and casually asked me how I was doing. Much to his surprise, I answered: "Well, Norbert, I am not very happy but have decided to just keep my mouth shut, do the show, take my money and go home!" "Oh," he said, "I'm sorry to hear that and what is it that's bothering you?" I told him in some detail and in reply, he said "Ah, I think I understand," but then he quickly added, "have you met Yvonne's understudy?" At that question, a small ray of hope flickered in my brain and I answered, "No, I didn't even know she had one." Without further ado he said, "Come with me and I will introduce you." So I happily followed him into the big rehearsal hall where all the singers and dancers were hard at work, and there, in the far corner of the room, sat a small figure.

I had never believed in the old saying "love at first sight," but in my mind this was sure something very much like it! As I looked at that small figure in the corner across that crowded room, I swear to you that I saw an aura around her which boded something very special. So, following Norbert, I was introduced.

When we shook hands, I truly felt an electric shock, and when I took her into the next room to show her the blocking of our first scene, I could have lit up the room with the flow I was feeling. Much later I found out that Mary Lynne Metternick was having similar feelings, perhaps not as profoundly as mine, but stirrings, nonetheless.

As we continued to rehearse, there came a point where I was to kiss the lady, so I warned her what was coming and proceeded to bend down to accomplish the deed. Our lips touched (all in character, of course!) and I knew I was a goner! A warm glow spread over me and I knew I was blushing, and all from just a peck that was called for in the script! What lay ahead if and when we actually got around to a real, personal kiss? I was determined to find out! Soon!

Now, of course, rehearsals were a pleasure and I looked forward to them each day. They had scheduled a number of preview performances in the next week or so, and Yvonne was still not prepared. She came in each day with a doctor's excuse about a sore throat or a pulled muscle, so it turned out that Mary Lynne would have to do the show—to my delight.

Right here, I hasten to add that Yvonne was a charming lady, but she just didn't seem to be too interested in doing the show, so the few times she did it before the official opening was really an adventure for me and the cast. I really had to be on my toes because I never quite knew what she would say for her line and, therefore, what my answer would be.

For instance, in one scene she had to change her dress so as to entice me to misbehave, thus getting me into a compromising position. In one preliminary show she got to this scene and came out with "I think I shall change into my BLUE JEANS," and the show was set in 1890!

We managed to get through it a few times, but Mary Lynne did more shows than Yvonne did and stuck to the script so it played more like CAN-CAN than the YVONNE DeCARLO show!

We did get through a number of rehearsals and the gang of producers decided that it was good enough to open officially with Yvonne in the lead role, which was what their contract with the hotel called for, so open we did.

The show went quite well and got good reviews, but soon Yvonne was reverting to her old ways with the doctor's excuse for a sore throat or whatever, and Mary Lynne would have to do the show. That certainly was fine with me, as I was falling more in love with her every day. I'm sure I pushed too fast and too far and she, although intrigued, wasn't ready for all my smothering attention.

We had moved from Motel Hell and the cast had spread out around town. ML and I had rented condos in the same building, though not together, and that made it easier for me to pursue my fair lady. However, she insisted on "her space" and I had to be satisfied with as much time as she would give me outside of performances.

The 1980s.

Very soon the producers and Yvonne came to an amicable agree-ment that she would leave the show and the question was who would replace her? They had already been auditioning other "names" for the part, but I went to my one producer friend and pleaded the case of Mary Lynne to take over which, ultimately, was what happened!

A lovely thing had been happening, which I'm sure helped with my plea for Mary Lynne. Each night she performed, when she came to the part where she walked to the end of the runway right out in the middle of the audience to sing "I Love Paris," she absolutely stopped the show! And then, out of the darkness, a hotel waiter would appear with a single rose which he formally presented to her. (We found out later that it came from the hotel management!) And it happened every time she sang that song, certainly an indication that the hotel people loved Mary Lynne's work! Of course that

Russ and Dorothy Collins on a personal appearance.

helped, and I was delighted when they made their decision and, obviously, so were a lot of other people because the show settled down for a seventh-month run. And this from an original four-week contract!

During the run I was able to persuade ML that I was really serious. It took some doing, believe me, but in my mind it was well worth it! I guess I proved a worthy suitor because she, and the cast, finally accepted the fact that we were a "couple," much to my relief!

A wonderful event took place one night when Bob Fosse, the great choreographer, and Gwen Verdon, the great dancer, who were the parents of Nicole, one of our dancers, came down to see her in the show. Now, I had worked with Bob years before when he was a guest performer on the *Hit Parade* and we had become good friends so when he came to our show he greeted me warmly which validated me in the eyes of the cast. They had never quite accepted me as a real performer as my credentials were "only" in TV and movies, not Broadway. However, after Bobby's hug, I was looked at with new eyes and felt a lot better for it.

After the show closed ML and I went back to New York to decide where we were going and how we would get there—wherever that might be. This began a three-year period which was spent between New York and California. I kept asking her to marry me and she kept saying she needed more time. We kept the airlines busy with my flying to New York and her flying to Hollywood. And during the in-between periods, well, it's no wonder that the price of AT&T stock went up sharply!

One day I had a call inviting me to take part in an inter-island "Hit Parade" cruise in Hawaii. They would fly each of us Hit Paraders first class, round trip, give us the cruise, pay each of us $1,500, and we would each do one show on "our" night during the week. A splendid offer, I thought, especially as ML had agreed to go with me, and so Snooky and Florence, Gisele and Bob, and Russell and Mary Lynne were on their way. Unfortunately, Dorothy Collins was ill and couldn't come with us, but we made a merry crew just the same!

During "my" night I was determined to include ML in my show and so our nightclub career began. It began "cute" you might say. I had the idea of seating ML in the audience and during the number when I went out into the audience to sing "close-up and personal" to the ladies, I would bring her back up on stage with me. While I was talking and exclaiming about her to the crowd, she would take the mike from me and begin singing a song of her own behind my back. It was all rehearsed, of course, but the audience didn't catch on for a while! Great fun, especially when the song turned into a duet!

The captain of the ship was ringside and ML got an inspiration out of the blue. His name was Captain Woo (a Chinese-American) and the song she sang was "It Had to Be You," so at the finish she leaned over his table, looked deep into his eyes, and in her high, clear soprano sang, "It had to be WOO!" Brought the house down, of course, and she became the toast of the ship. Another night we had dinner at the captain's table and met the great quarterback of the San Francisco 49ers, Joe Montana, which was a thrill. More for me than Mary Lynne, I guess.

The cruise ended all too soon, but we were able to spend another couple of weeks in Honolulu with some friends who lived on the island, so it turned out to be a wonderful trip and memory. Now it was time to return to the Mainland and our back-and-forth-ing across the continent.

I had some friends, Jackie and Norm, who lived in a beautiful home in Brentwood, near UCLA, and they had traded their home for a month with a couple from Paris, so we made arrangements to rent rooms from them for the last week of their month in Paris—a sort of pre-marriage honeymoon—because, wonder of wonders, I had finally convinced Mary Lynne to marry me! Our plan was to come back to New York, after Paris, close out her apartment, get married in Long Island at her sister Janet's house, and then return to California.

We had a wonderful week in Paris even though the weather was overcast and cold and everyone was out of town for summer vacation. It was August and that's when the natives leave town. Not knowing any better, though, we had a great time riding the Metro, eating dinner in the Eiffel Tower and other fancy restaurants and, especially, going up to Montmarte, which is the artists' area and is the setting for the musical *Can-Can*—which, romantically, is where we met! Naturally, Mary Lynne positioned me on a beautiful old bench and sang "I Love Paris" to me amidst tears and smiles.

Then we climbed up a very old, worn, winding stairway in the beautiful Sacre Coeur church until it felt like we were in the clouds and overlooking a great sweep of Paris with the Eiffel Tower in the middle distance. Romance, indeed!

Leaving Paris was a joke! None of us spoke French and, somehow, I was elected to make arrangements for a cab over the phone with a Frenchman who spoke very little English but understood the address I gave him. He showed up to take the four of us, with ALL of our luggage, to Orly Airport. How he managed to pack everything in his little Fiat I will never know, but he did. It was probably worth it to him because when he dropped us off, Norm and I emptied our pockets of all the French coins we had accumulated and dropped them into his eager hands. I have no idea what we gave him but he was very pleased!

Back in New York we quickly got into the pace of that great city and went ahead with arrangements for the wedding. Suffice it to say, it was two weeks of bedlam, back and forth to Long Island, selling ML's furniture and settling her lease, plane tickets to California, arranging for an Irish Justice of the Peace to perform the ceremony, inviting guests, getting the caterer for the reception dinner, signing up for our license, and attending several parties!

But it was not to be a smooth operation because ML, again feeling some trepidation about leaving New York and all the contacts and friends she had made in her twelve years there, still had some doubts about the huge change it would make in her life to marry me and move to the coast.

I really can't say that I blamed her, but I had had it with all the delays and disappointments we had gone through, so I stamped my little foot, put on my best pouty expression, and made an ultimatum: if I walked out the door, that was it! I would never be back!

Thereupon, I got dressed, packed my suitcase, and angry and fearful, waited by her front door for the deadline to pass. Two minutes before that fateful moment ML relented and rushed into my arms amid tears and sobs, on both our parts, and everything was on "GO" again!

Hooray and hallelujah! So, it came about that in Janet and Don's lovely and very crowded home, the beautiful marriage took place. We had managed to gather together most of ML's family as well as many of her New York friends to celebrate with us and, midst much laughter, singing and drinking of METTERNICH champagne—yes, an old family brand—we FINALLY accomplished the deed!!

The next day we flew off for the West one more time with cheerful hearts and great anticipation as to what the future held for us!

Chapter 24
The Denouement

My one-bedroom apartment was a lot more crowded with the addition of ML's things, although I was in seventh heaven at having captured my beautiful prize. Fortunately, ML was a great "pack rat." After living in New York, she knew more ways to save space than I ever knew existed and was able to put everything in order so we could settle down to living.

A little sidenote here: I had lived in this apartment house for a few years and had a casual, nodding acquaintance with all the other tenants, but after my bride moved in it became a whole different thing. She immediately made friends with everyone and, suddenly, we had a flood of visitors, as well as doing our own visiting, so our social life became very busy. Such were her warmth and openness that it negated my propensities for being a recluse. Bless her for that!

On the business side, things were a bit slow. There were still narrations to do and pageants to emcee, but TV was hard to come by and, although we tried hard to find work for ML, that change of coasts was difficult, at best. She did do a musical, *Nite Club Confidential*, in Scottsdale, Arizona, for two months, and also became a big band singer with occasional jobs around the area. Great fun! On my side we did have the pageants and fashion shows to fall back on and that provided some work. But now there was a new possibility, our being a singing team, and that was more successful.

For instance, we flew to Florida to the Clearwater Country Club for a very successful engagement, and I still laugh about an incident there. After the show we stood near the doorway as the audience filed out to thank them for coming and a dear lady of about 88 or so suddenly stopped in front of me and exclaimed, "Your wife is a lot better than you are!" I

The millenium.

quickly agreed and she continued on out, whereupon we broke into gales of laughter. I quickly have to say that my throat problem had started, so I wasn't at my best, to say the least!

Anyway, the next year we returned to Florida to play three Moose Lodges and had the promise from our booker of returning to them, as well as several other venues that he handled. So, that whole situation looked very promising for us.

However, a totally unexpected black cloud had appeared on the horizon. Just above, I mentioned my "throat problem." I had been having a bit of trouble with my voice, and it was becoming more and more difficult for me to sing. My health was fine, but the voice became weaker and weaker—an alarming feeing! No matter that I took very good care of myself, physically, I grew hoarser and hoarser until it finally became necessary to seek medical help.

That began a nightmare of medical tests, semi-operations and consultations that lasted five years. I went to UCLA Medical Center, Columbia-Presbyterian Hospital in New York, to several independent doctors, as well as several holistic healers, acupuncturists, hypnotists—you name it, I tried it! But, unfortunately, nothing seemed to help.

I still managed to do some pageant and fashion show emceeing and had even gotten Mary Lynne involved in both those fields, but every show I did was a major effort, and I knew the end was near for my performing days. What a bleak feeling it was to know that I could no longer do the only thing I had done for my entire life! I struggled through a big benefit show we were doing together in Keokuk, Iowa, (ML's hometown, incidentally), and right then made the decision that I was through, unless a miracle happened—something that I am still waiting for!

To put a name to this evil thing: it's called "spasmodic dysphonia," and it affects more people than one would think. There are three kinds, all in the same family, and that makes it harder to recognize. I have the "breathy" kind (abductor) and cannot achieve any resonance, so I sound like the Godfather most of the time. The second type is "tight" kind (adductor) where one sounds like he is strangling, and the third is a tremolo sounding like a heavy case of the hiccups. The good news is that it's not life-threatening, doesn't hurt and it's NOT cancer; SD just makes it difficult, almost impossible, to communicate.

For instance, talking on the phone is a chore or being at a party is very difficult because the ambient noise in the room, the music, the cocktail chatter, all make it hard to be heard. The constant question, "I'm sorry, what did you say?," is hard both on me and the person I'm talking with. Even Mary Lynne gets frustrated once in a while because she can't hear or understand me! And I think I'm speaking quite normally! I know I'm a lot better off than many people, but it simply means that my career has come to a screeching halt and that's hard to take after so many years.

However, life goes on and one adjusts to it! We decided to move out of Hollywood as long as I couldn't narrate or emcee anymore, and it was getting more crowded and smoggier by the day, so we began looking for places to live. We tried Florida and Northern California before coming down to Palm Springs and, after much debate, found a place that suited our needs and so settled down in the Desert.

In the more than 12 years we've been here we've been doing both the good and the bad about this place. Unfortunately the air quality that was so clear and beautiful is gradually succumbing to the smog that is filtering through the mountain passes, and we're feeling the effects of that. Also, the small-town feeling that we loved at first is being lost in the welter of people who seem to be moving here. Also, the hot summer months of August and September are sometimes unbearable! However, when the weather is fine it still seems like heaven on earth, and we love the home we bought and on which we have lavished our love and decorating talents. So one weighs the good with the bad and forges ahead with life.

Mary Lynne has become very successful in theaters here and is becoming a very well-known personality in the Desert, starring in such shows as *Mame, Hello, Dolly!, The Cocktail Hour, Equus, Dames at Sea*, the female version of *The Odd Couple*, and many others. She also does many concert-style shows at country clubs. At present she is working on three different productions at once! I have done some directing at different theaters here and find it gratifying, to an extent. Yet, I would love to perform again, but that's up to the Good Lord.

In the meantime, I can help ML do her shows and have become a champion line-cuer and book-holder, which does help her. I also make dinner when she has to get to rehearsals or shows or publicity stints on radio or TV (I knew that the cooking I learned so long ago would come in handy!), so I generally just try to keep things going. Not bad for an octogenarian, and I'm looking forward to many more years of being involved.

Fortunately, my health is good (except for my throat) and my interest in and desire for the theater has not diminished. That seems to me to be the secret of retirement, forced or otherwise, to stay involved and keep one's energy and interest going. I have the advantage of having been a so-called "star" and, much to my surprise, still receive a lot of fan mail from both here and abroad, and I do answer it myself. I have no idea of what the future may bring but as long as I have a loving wife, good health, and energy, well, for what more can I ask!?

I devoutly want to thank all my fans who still maintain an interest in my life and who have been so wonderful throughout my career. It helps to know that other people care about what happens to you, and I find it gratifying that so many of my "fans" have turned into "friends."

My feeling has always been that in order to be successful, one needs talent, some training, and a whole lot of LUCK! You must be in the right place at the right time but then be prepared, and able, to deliver. I think I've had my share of luck throughout my life and am eternally grateful for that. I have been able to store up a lot of memories and a lot of experience and knowledge that I can pass along to others through coaching and directing. So, in spite of my throat, I feel that I have made, and can still make, some kind of contribution in the field that I have loved so well and for so long.

Who knows what may happen in the future. With my "child bride," Mary Lynne, keeping me hopping with her activities and her love, I feel ready to face another millennium with hope and anticipation! And who knows, maybe that long hoped-for miracle will suddenly appear one fine day!

The Ladies

I decided to add a few more pages of interest—to me, at least. These varied subjects are random thoughts that I decided might as well be included in these memoirs.

The first thing I thought of, of course, was the many beautiful, talented, and exciting ladies I have had the pleasure of working with these many years. I thought I might make it a bit more titillating if I suggested that with SOME of these beauties there might have been a bit more than just a working relationship. Not being a kiss-and-tell-type, I shall leave it to you to decide if that was even possible, and, if so, who it (or they) might possibly be!

Remember, I've been lucky all my life! And, that having been said, here is my list of Ladies I Have Worked With!

BETTE DAVIS, ANN SHERIDAN, MARTHA RAYE, ANNE JEFFREYS, BRENDA MARSHALL, PATRICE MUNSEL, EDIE ADAMS, FAYE EMERSON, YVONNE DeCARLO, LILO, JUNE VALLI, DOROTHY COLLINS, GISELE MacKENZIE, ARLENE DAHL, AND JULIET PROWSE.

To continue: CHITA RIVERA, POLLY BERGEN, CAROL CHANNING, JUNE LOCKHART, CLORIS LEACHMAN, JANE RUSSELL, JANE WYATT, GALE STORM, ZASU PITTS, KAREN BLACK, PATTI PAGE, EYDIE GORME, MARGE CHAMPION,

BILLIE BURKE, and DORIS DAY.

And others: ETHEL BARRYMORE, DAGMAR, ELINOR DONAHUE, MARILYN MAXWELL, ADELE MARA, BARBARA BRITTON, ELEANOR PARKER, MARY WICKES and, would you believe, ZSA ZSA GABOR!

As I read over this list, I feel very proud and lucky to have known and worked with so many lovely ladies!

Addenda 2
Bubba

Most everyone likes a dog story, yes? After Barbara, the kids, and I moved into the house on Laurel Terrace Drive, they found a dog next door who had just had puppies and nothing would do but that we have one. So, we got one. He was a cockapoo, a nice mixture, all black and with nice short hair that didn't shed. So far, so good! There were promises from the girls that they would take care of him, feed him, clean up after him, etc., but you know how those things go and, eventually, he really became "my" dog. Which was okay with me.

Anyway, he turned out to be a wonderful dog. I know anyone who owns a dog thinks his pup is the cutest, smartest, and best behaved one around, but Bubba really was! We had to be careful what we said around him because he understood, yes, *understood*, what we were talking about. Honest!

Fetching the paper each morning became a routine that he loved. He would dash out to the driveway, pick it up and have a wonderful time delivering it to my feet. Except on Sunday—that was a problem. *The Los Angeles Times* becomes a monster on Sunday, and it was actually bigger than Bubba! So, watching him try to pick it up and move it was hilarious, but not to him. The bigger it was, the more determined he was to get it in the house. I finally had to rescue it from his slavering jaws so I would have something left to read.

Why do small dogs hate deliverymen, postmen, or anyone in uniform? Bub was no exception. One morning I was out in the yard working among the flowers and he was right by my side when all at once he started barking and carrying on and, sure enough, the postman was there. I quieted the dog and started chatting with the man when, very deliberately and with great dignity, Bubba slowly walked over to him, took his time, and lifted his leg! When I saw what was happening I screamed and stopped him, but the damage was done. Bubba, completely unfazed, slowly walked away and disappeared around the corner of the house, with, I swear, a smile on his face while I stood gasping and trying to apologize! Looking back, it was very funny, but not at the time!

Needless to say, he had many endearing qualities and became a treasured member of the family. He was a loyal and dependable little guy and we loved him.

At any rate, time went by and we finally came to our breakup. Barb and the girls moved out and Bub and I were left in the house to decide what to do. First, I wanted to find a good home for him, and just try that some time! I called everyone I knew who might be remotely interested but with no results. I advertised, called any organization with "dog" in their title, still no results.

Finally, a very nice young lady I was dating said she would take him if I would take care of his expenses: food, the vet, and the like. I jumped at the chance and so he was adopted and all went well until the day he accidentally dirtied in the backseat of her car! That was it. She wouldn't keep him anymore, and after much maneuvering he was adopted again, this time by her cleaning lady with promises of much love and care for Bub. She had a son and a fenced-in yard and all would be well.

Two months went by and on a cold, rainy February morning I received a phone call from what we used to call a "pound" saying they had my dog there and would I come and get him! I replied that I had no dog but they insisted that my name was on his license tag and I should come and get him.

So I went down to a poorer section of L.A. and found the "pound." There, sitting in an open pen surrounded by a number of other wet, dirty miscreants, was Bubba. He sat by himself in a corner and was very angry at the world, as who could blame him! Without him seeing me, I went back in the office to retrieve him, but the little Hitler who ran the place would have none of it. He demanded proof that I was indeed the dog's owner, and this after him calling me and telling me I was. He then left the room and I stood there wondering what to do when a little black girl, an angel, appeared. She was a worker in the office and had seen the whole thing transpire and was there to help. She suggested that I call the vet who treated Bub and thereby prove I was who I said I was. That is what happened and how I was able to pay the ransom and spring Bub.

Now I was free to get him home, if he would have me. So back out into the rain I went and, this time, I called his name. He was galvanized instantly! Have me back? He practically went through the fence! I took the little piece of string the girl had given me—had to have a leash, you know—and attached it to his collar and off we went to the car. He was wet and filthy dirty but beside himself with joy. He talked his head off and when we got in the car he buried his head in my shirt and kept talking. Pure joy!

When we got back to the apartment, I ran a bathtub full of warm water and put him in. He smelled to high heaven and the dirt and scum that came off him was unbelievable, but he was really enjoying himself and was turning back into the playful pup he once was. I scrubbed him as best as I could and got him somewhat presentable and he thanked me over and over by doing all his old tricks and licking me everywhere he could reach. Tears were streaming down my face by this time as I called the vet and made an appointment for the next morning to have him looked over.

I had noticed a number of lumps and ugly little scabs on his body and feared the worst. When the vet looked him over, sure enough, he had some alarming symptoms, of what I didn't know and didn't want to know. I explained my dilemma to the doc and got nothing by sympathy, only. I couldn't keep the dog in the apartment and couldn't find anyone else who would take him and was stumped! So, talking it over with the vet, I had to make the hard decision to put Bubba down.

He assured me it was instantaneous and would not hurt in the least, so, as I held my buddy in my arms and before I could even get ready for it, the shot had been given and Bubba's head fell on my shoulder. And it was over, except for the nightmares I had, and the dreams I still have, and the mountain of regret I still have. One of the hardest things I ever had to do.

As a footnote, I told Barbara, my ex, about it and what a trauma it had been and was, to which she replied, "Oh, well, he was only a dog!"

Not quite, Barb, not quite!

Addenda 3
The Training Film

While I was in the Army and after a year in service I was suddenly alerted that I was to be shipped out to California for detached service. I had no idea what it was all about and my orders simply read that I was to report to a major in Beverly Hills on or about a certain date. So, dutifully, I packed my gear, got on a train, a troop train, and embarked on quite an adventure. After about a week of train travel, I arrived at Union Station in L.A. on a Friday afternoon. I immediately called the number I had been given and got a second lieutenant who had the "duty" that night. He said they were expecting me but didn't need me until Monday, so when he heard that I had previously lived in L.A. he told me to find a place to stay and report in on Monday!

I didn't need to be told twice and immediately began casting about in my mind as to where I could stay. Thinking that I might at least get a weekend bed I decided to call my lady friend in Hollywood and see what happened. Her immediate answer was that I should "come right over." So I hopped a cab and was greeted with open arms and told I could stay with her for a while. Her aunt, with whom she was sharing a two-bedroom apartment, was leaving the next morning for a year's stay out of town! So I had found a temporary home at least.

On Monday I reported to the major's office and was told that I was there to star in a major training film that was to be shot at Warner Bros. studios and to report out there the following day. Great news! It turned out that the major was a friend, the producer of the last film I had made before going into service. He had requested me to do this film, and so I was back and at work just where I had left off.

I called my friend to whom I sold my car and he let me borrow it back for as long as I needed it, so that problem was solved. I went to Army HQs where they took care of rations and quarters for detached service people and that, too, was taken care of, so I was just about set up and ready to go to work.

I reported to Warners and got a script and shooting schedule, then went back to the apartment and sat down with my friend. I had managed to stop at an Army facility to buy a bottle of vodka to take home with me where we sat down to work out the necessary arrangements: what rent I would pay and how much food I would provide, etc., and suddenly it felt like I wasn't in the Army at all!

Most of the film was shot out on location at the Warners' ranch in Calabasas, deep in the Valley. They had a great set-up with all the necessary weapons, trucks and a couple of platoons of actual Army troops who had been detached to lay the real fighting troops in the film. Our director was Breezy Eason, an old-time "chase" director who was wonderful at action work and, of course, that is what this film would mostly be.

The reason this film was so important was that it showed a young man (me) preparing for his first battle and then going into that battle. They tried to show the ugly side of war, the explosions, bodies, the blood from wounds, a tank being hit and blowing up, burning men screaming and trying to get out of it, a man's friend being hit and dying at his side, an ambulance filled with wounded and stuck in a giant mud hole, all the terrible things a soldier might encounter on a battlefield. It was an attempt to dull the shock that was sure to come when a new soldier was in his first fire-fight.

On the eve of the battle several of us soldiers had gathered together and were discussing what we faced the next day. Thus, the emotional and psychological side of battle was also brought out. All in all, it was a powerful film and one that all trainees had to see. It was an effort to help prepare men for the vicious and terrible experience they would be facing.

There were lighter moments, of course. I was lying in a foxhole preparing for a scene one afternoon when a young second lieutenant (one of the regular troops) came by and started talking with me. He wanted to know what I thought of the Army and its equipment and methods. Obviously, he didn't know that I was "in" and I played along and let him think I was just an actor. That way I didn't have to salute him...ha!

We had a group of stunt men assigned to the picture, but I tried to do as many of my own action things as possible. I had a lot of running through very rough terrain, avoiding planted explosive pots, diving into shell holes, as well as a couple of big fights with bayonets to do and, if I do say so myself, managed to do them very well. I'll admit that I did intermix some of the bayonet fighting with the stunt double, however. He did the rough stuff and I did the close-ups! 'Twas ever thus in the movies!

This went on for about three months and finally they said it was finished. However, I did have to wait around in case they needed any retakes, which I happily did. During that time off I made some phone calls to Ft. Roach which was the old Hal Roach Studio that the Air Force had taken over. A lot of well-known names were stationed out there—Ronald Reagan, for one. I knew the lieutenant who was doing the casting for the Air Force, so I asked him if he needed any actors for any forthcoming films. He said as soon as I was free from the picture I had just done to call him and he would definitely use me. So in about two weeks I did get the "all clear" from the Army, made the call, and was immediately cast in not one, but three, Air Force films. After all the official paper work was finished, I had been put on further detached service but this time assigned to the Air Force.

My first film for the Air Force was called *Pilotage and Dead Reckoning for Pilots*, not exactly a drawing-room comedy, but a necessary lot of information for real pilots. This one was a "nuts and bolts"-type of pic. Ah, but the third, was special. We were sent on location to Walla Walla, Washington, where there was a big B-17 bomber air base because this was a film on B-17 teamwork. I was to play the bombardier and that was very special because the ultra-secret Norden bombsight was just being released to the air fleet.

The first time I was to see this bombsight was quite a show. They didn't know that I had been cleared for "secret," so I was accompanied by a captain with a sidearm down a long flight of stairs into a triple-locked cement room where the sight was stored. With great care the captain unlocked the box to show it to me and explain how it was used. I looked at it with a bit of curiosity but some indifference because all this was useless. All they would have had to do was to tell me the general motions I would use to line up the sight and let it go at that. No one could tell just what I was doing, but now it was official. Anyway, I couldn't have given away any secrets because I didn't understand a bit of it!

I had met a young redheaded pilot who was hanging around our set. He had cracked up one of the 17s and, it having just been repaired, he was about to take it up for a test flight and wondered if I might like to go along. Being young and dumb, I said that sure I'd like to go, and did. He put me in the copilot seat and after we were safely in level flight at the proper altitude asked me if I'd like to fly it. Again, being y and d, I allowed as how I'd like that and so took the wheel, held it for a while, and then was able to say that I had "flown" a B-17! Quite an experience!

However, all good things must come to an end, so we came back to Ft. Roach and my stint in the Air Force was over. Nothing for it but to return to the Army and leave my little home in Hollywood and return to New York and the Signal Corps. I had managed to eke out six months, though, so it was a grand adventure.

One final note on the training film. A new edict came down from Washington that any troops who had been in the Army for two years without having been in battle would now have to take a refresher training course. So a group of us from SCPC was shipped down to Red Bank, New Jersey, for that course. A regular Army first lieutenant was assigned to put us through this training which included firing a lot of guns, going through a lot of drills and procedures and, best of all, seeing training films! Most of us in the group had either written, narrated, or produced these films.

One day we were marched to the post theater to see a film and, you guessed it, the film was the one I had just finished shooting! The lieutenant was sitting fairly near me in the theater and I could see him turn and look at me as the film ran on. I have to interject right here that he wasn't the brightest of men, as witness when the film was finished and we were lined up in the street again, he called me out of ranks and put me in charge of the unit! The power of film!

Addenda 4

Performance Resume

HIGH SCHOOL
Elizabeth the Queen	The Fool
Death Takes a Holiday	Death
Berkeley Square	Peter
Rosalinda (one-act)	

PENINSULA PLAYER
Tweedles

SAN MATEO JUNIOR COLLEGE
The Dover Road	Nicholas
And So to Bed	Sam. Pepys
Craig's Wife	Craig
Stage Door	Keith

PASADENA PLAYHOUSE
Cesare Borgia (one-act)	Borgia
The Boy Comes Home (one-act)	Boy
Oedipus Rex	
Hands Across the Sea	Butler
Ulysses Sailed By	Paul
Beware of Cats	Baron
The Frodii	
Merchant of Venice	Salario
The Deluge	Ham

Backdoor to Heaven (Jr. Musical)	Belial
Texas Nightingale	the son
See My Lawyer	Arthur
Tomorrow is a Woman	Brother
Breath of Kings	Louis XII
Everyman	Everyman
Merchant of Venice	Lorenzo
The Lady of Belmont	Lorenzo
Whistling for a Wind	soldier
Lost Horizon	Stage Manager
Kiss for Cinderella	Chorus
Bartholomew's Fair	
The Critic	Sir Dangle
The Way of the World	
Made in Heaven	Philip
The Turquoise Matrix	Steven
Mary Rose	Stephen

MOTION PICTURES

The Man Who Came to Dinner	Richard Stanley
Captains of the Clouds	Alabama
Wings for the Eagles	Pete Hanso
Always in My Heart	Red
Wallflower	
Deception	
That Way with Women	
Life with Father	
The High Wall	
Sealed Verdict	
Daredevils of the Sky	
The Checkered Coat	
John Loves Mary	
By the Light of the Silvery Moon	

TELEVISON

Lucky Strikes Hit Parade	(Six years starring)
Matinee Theater (2)	Peggy Lee…June Lockhart
	Svengali and the Blonde

	Carol Channing,
	Basil Rathbone
Have Gun-Will Travel (2)	Richard Boone
December Bride	Spring Byington
Border Patrol	Broderick Crawford
Rawhide (3)	Clint Eastwood
Gunsmoke	James Arness
Perry Mason (3)	Raymond Burr
Lock Up (2)	McDonald Carey
Buckskin	
This is Alice	
Banacek	
Marcus Welby, M.D. (3)	Robert Young
Mod Squad	
The FBI	Efrem Zimbalist, Jr.
Surfside 6	
Ichabod and Me	Robert Sterling
The Rogues	Gig Young
Day in Court	
Dragnet	Jack Webb
Line Up	
Baptist Films	
On the Strip	
Bell Telephone Hour	
Barbara Stanwyck (FBI)	
Patti Page	
Gale Storm (Oh, Susanna)	
Captain's Lady (pilot)	

COMMERCIALS
Lucky Strikes
Alka-seltzer
AT&T
Falstaff Beer
Cool Pops
Bell Telephone
Kool Cigarettes
Miller High Life Beer

THEATER PERFORMANCES

Can-Can – 5 productions	Lilo, Edie Adams, Patrice Munsel, Chita Rivera, Mary Lynne Metternich
Bells Are Ringing – 2 productions	Anne Jeffreys
1776	
Anything Goes	
Catch Me If You Can - 2 productions	Jane Russell
Mr. Roberts	Robert Fuller
Bye Bye Birdie	
Redhead	
Irma La Douce – 2 productions	Ruta Lee, Juliet Prowse
The Pleasure of His Company	Efrem Zimbalist, Jr.

Printed in the United States
28477LVS00005B/328-351